Cat Hair Everywhere

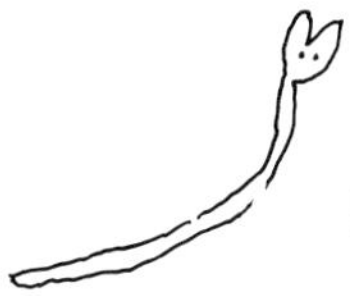

RON ELLSWORTH

CAPRA PRESS
Santa Barbara

Copyright ©1988 by Ron Ellsworth.
All rights reserved.
Printed in the United States of America.

LIBRARY OF CONGRESS CATALOGING-IN-PUBLICATION DATA
Ellsworth, Ron, 1945-
Cat hair everywhere / by Ron Ellsworth.
ISBN 0-88496-287-3 (pbk.) : $12.95
1. Cats—Caricatures and cartoons.
2. American wit and humor, Pictorial.   I. Title.
NC1429.E524A   1988   88-4700
741.5'973—dc19   CIP

CAPRA PRESS
Post Office Box 2068
Santa Barbara, California 93120

To Suzanne, David, and the following special furries:
Sweetpea, Mr. Grayson Proboscis, Pinky,
Butterbox, and Pumpkin the Piglet.

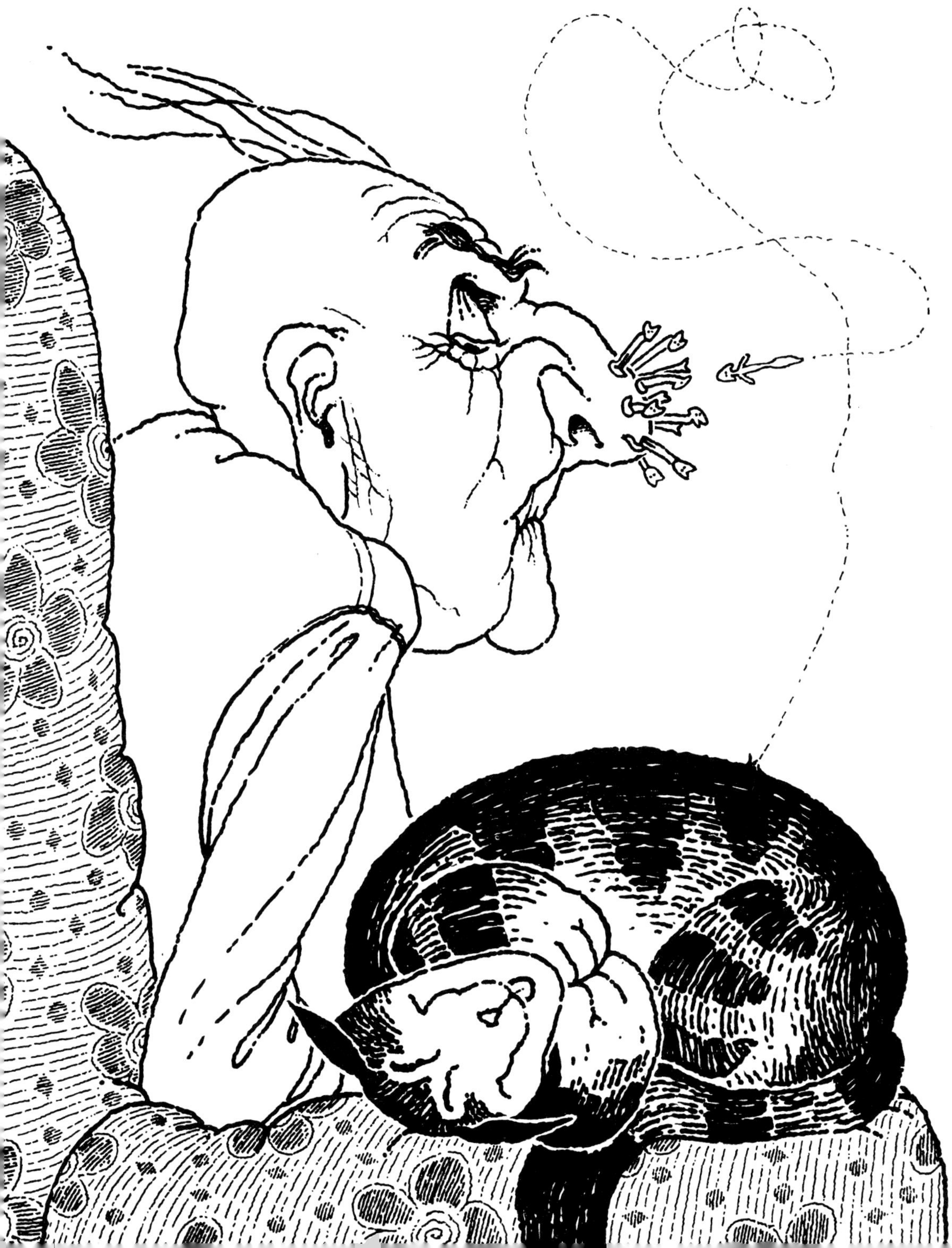

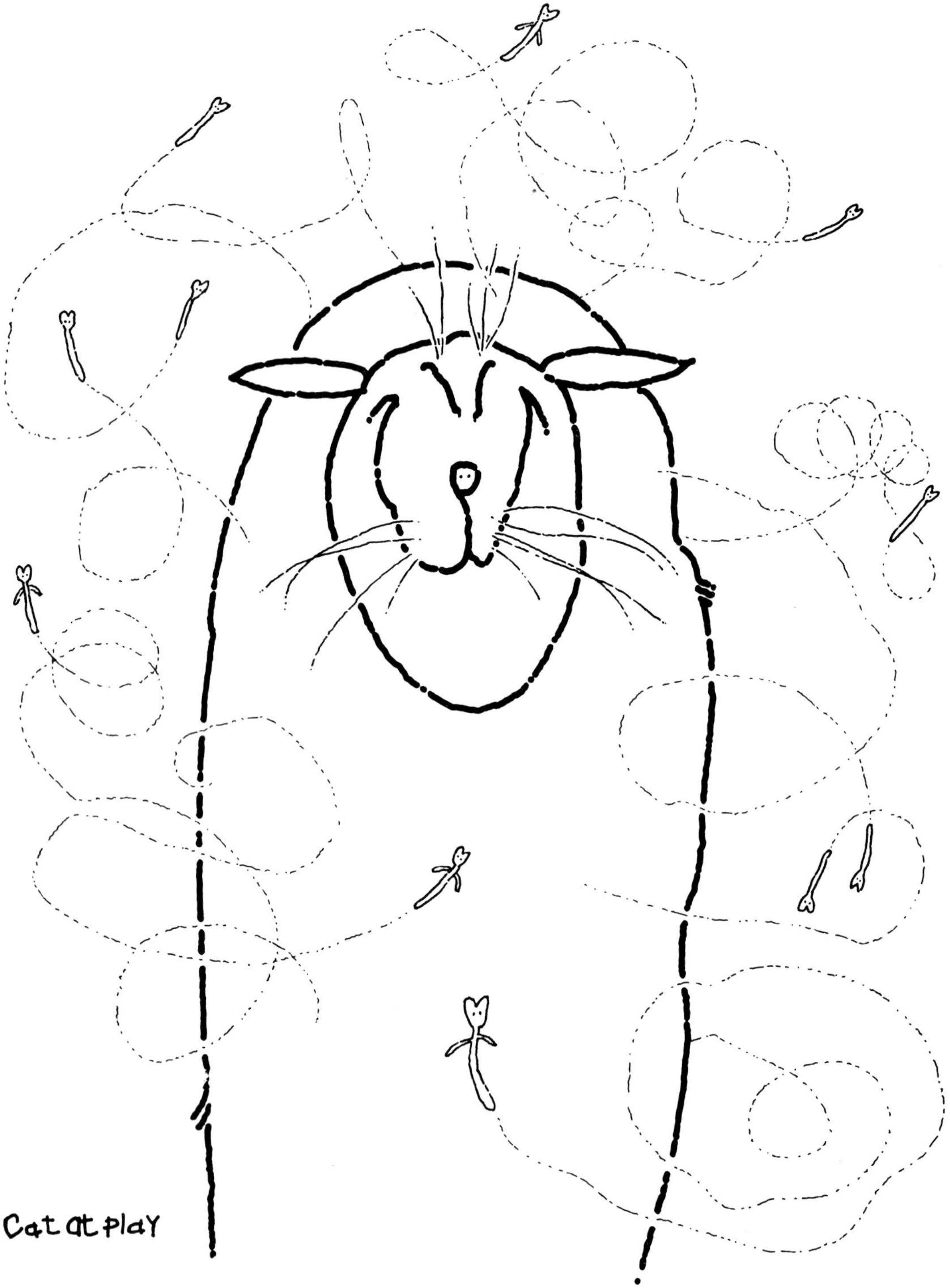

Cat at play

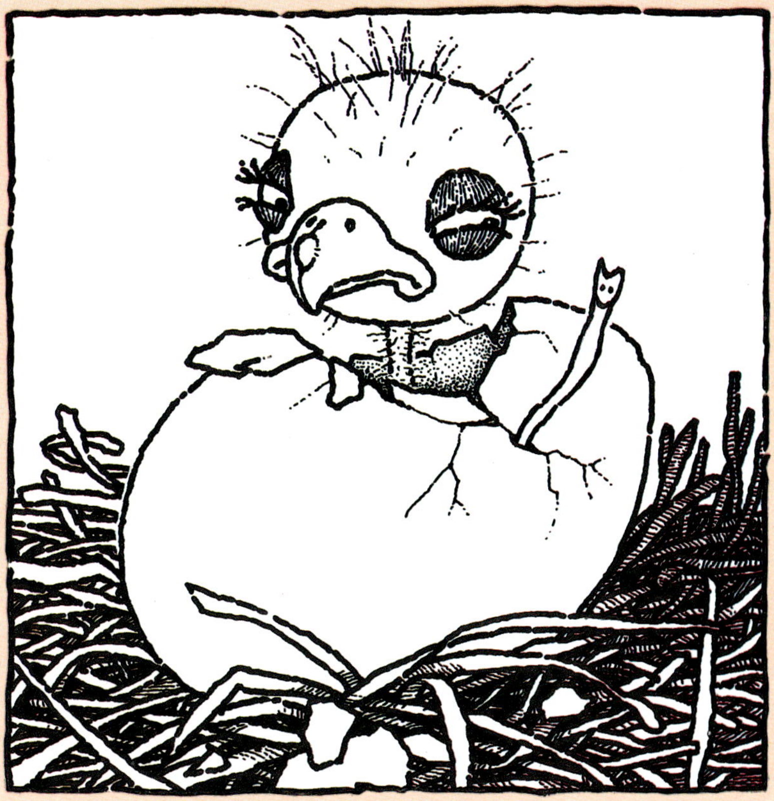

it's everywhere

Cat Lady

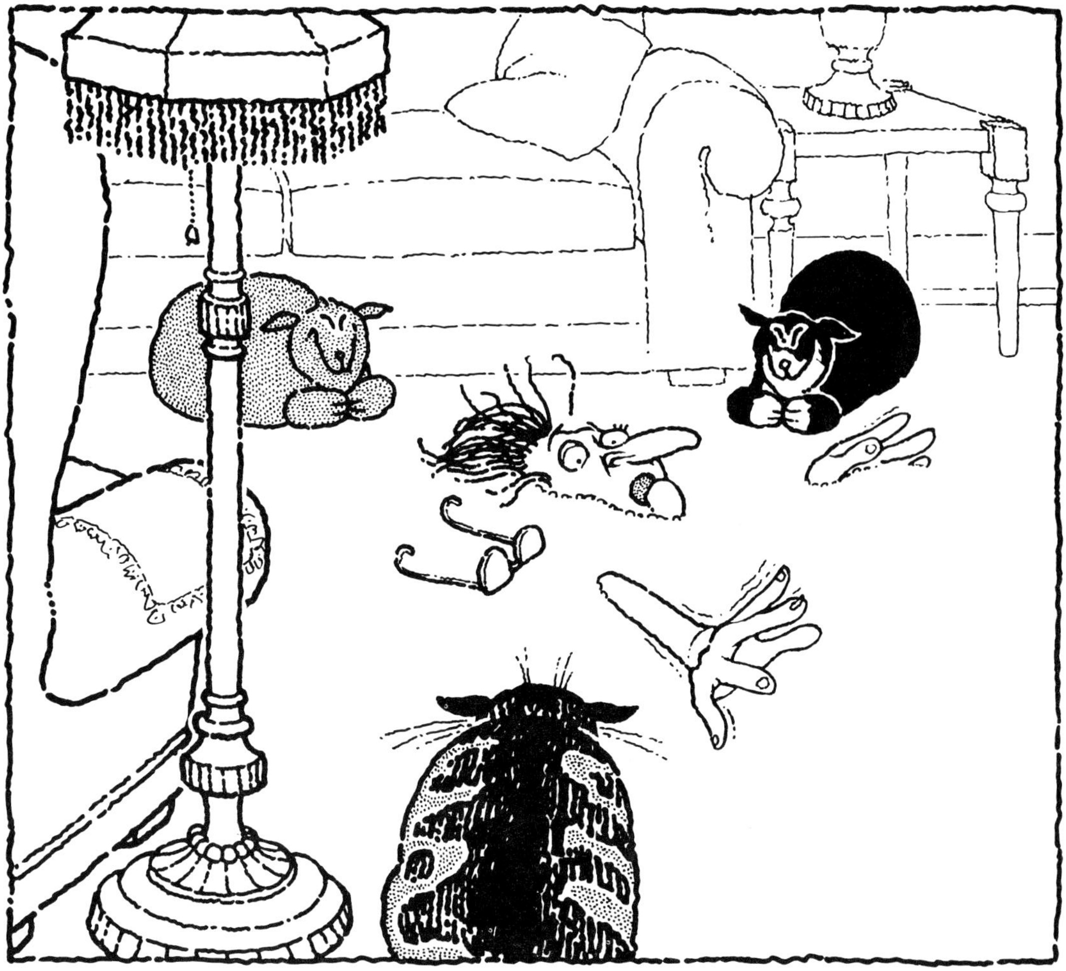

the burmeowda triangle

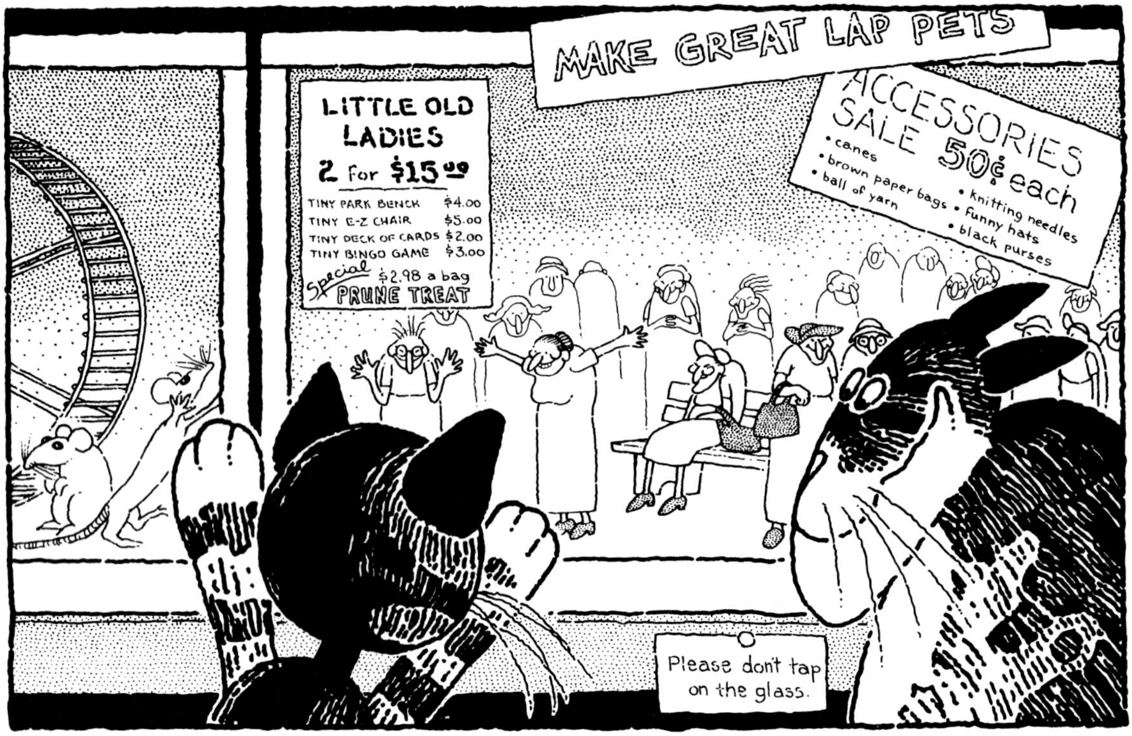
MAKE GREAT LAP PETS
LITTLE OLD LADIES
2 for $15.00
TINY PARK BENCH $4.00
TINY E-Z CHAIR $5.00
TINY DECK OF CARDS $2.00
TINY BINGO GAME $3.00
Special $2.98 a bag
PRUNE TREAT
ACCESSORIES SALE 50¢ each
• canes
• brown paper bags
• ball of yarn
• knitting needles
• funny hats
• black purses
Please don't tap on the glass.

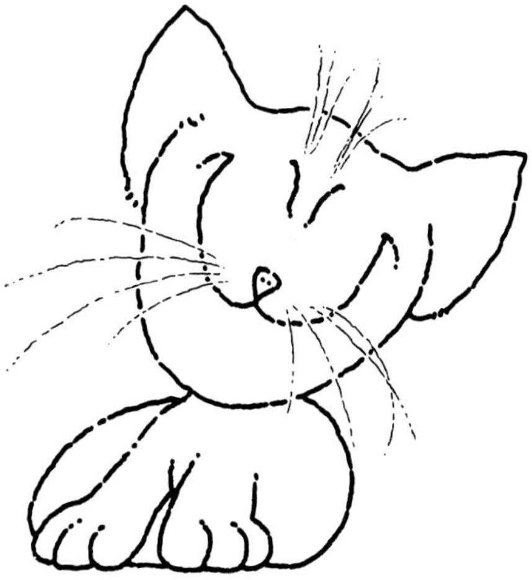

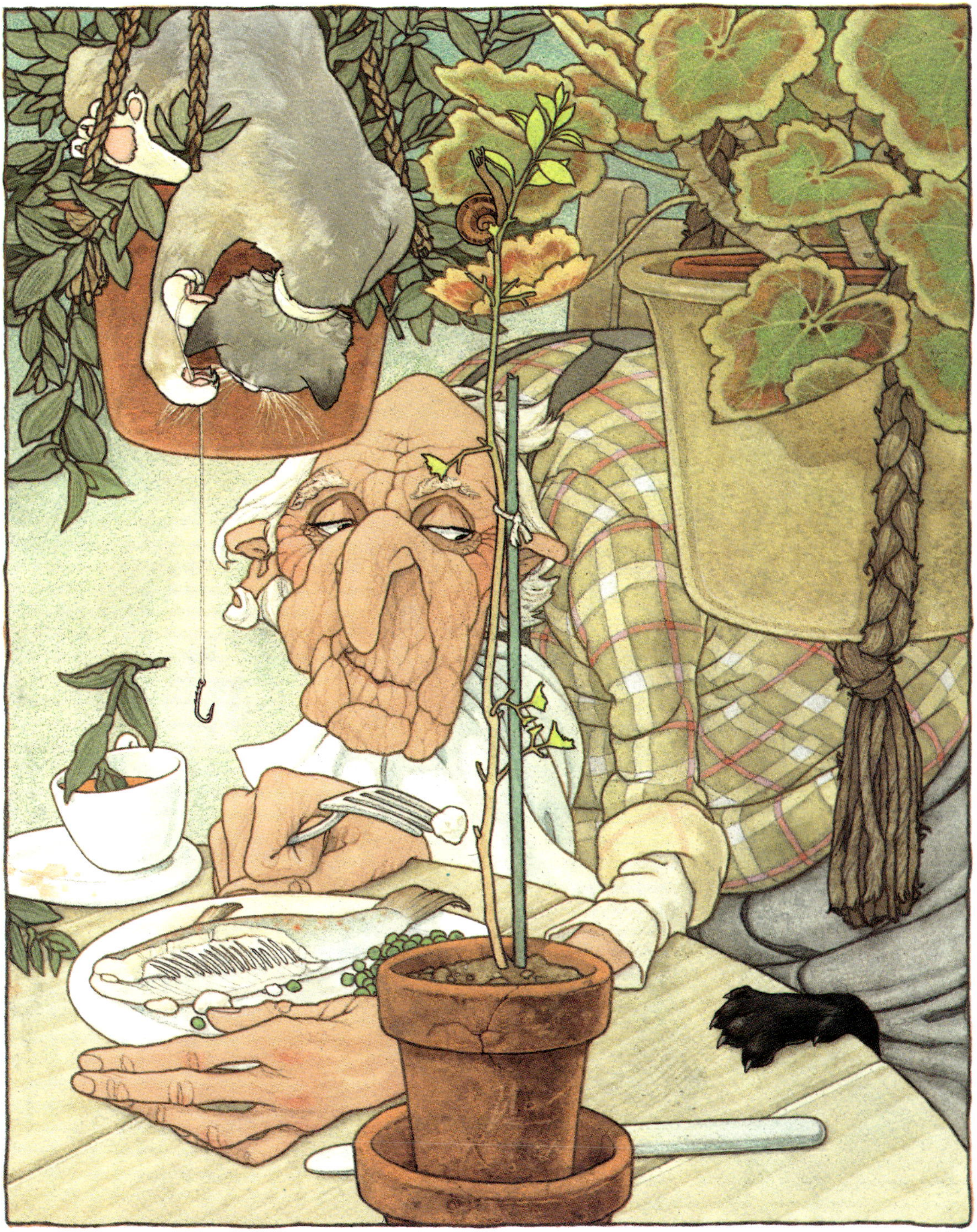

fish dinner

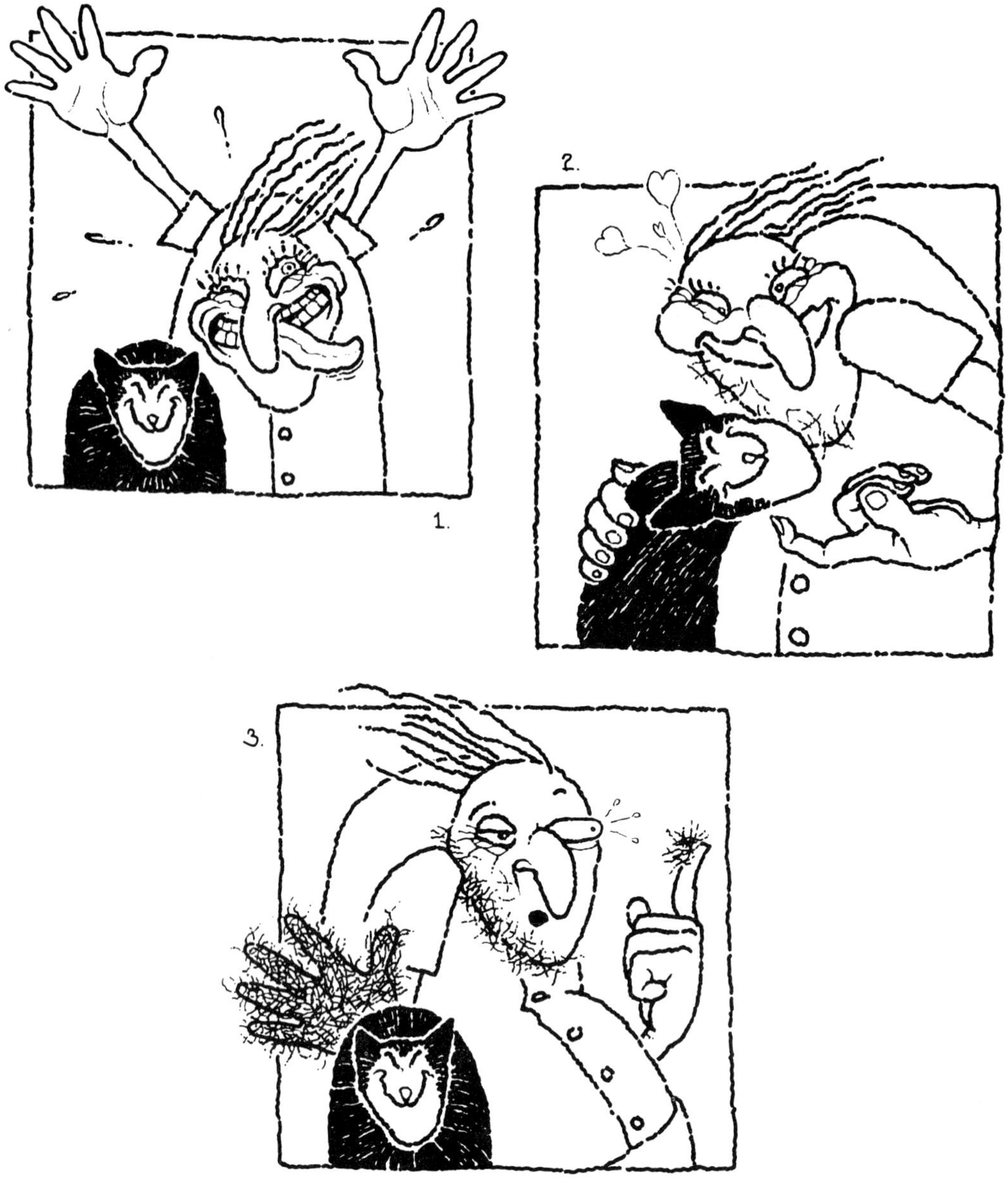
1.
2.
3.

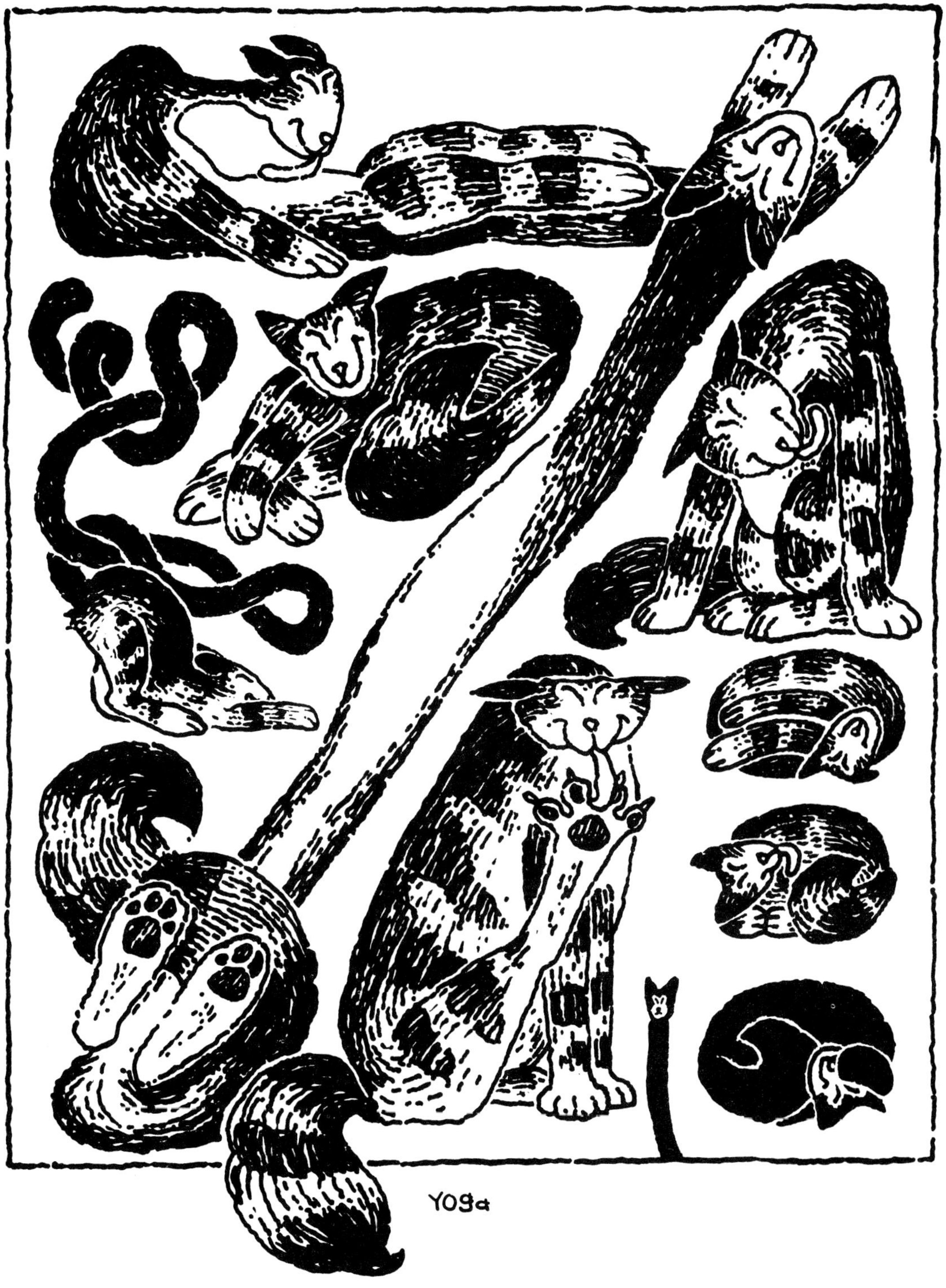

YOGA

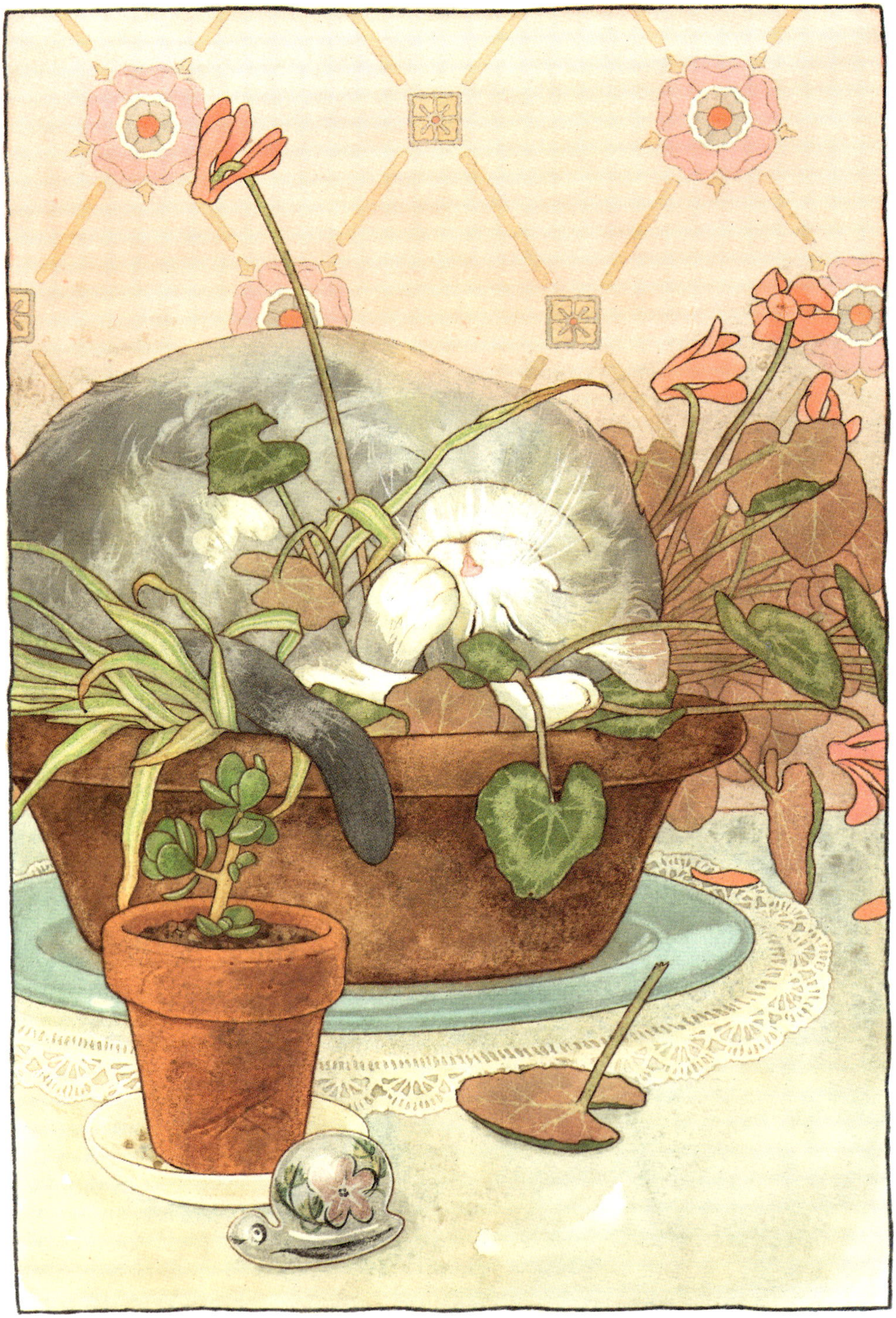

noodle takes a nap

cat bubbling over with joy

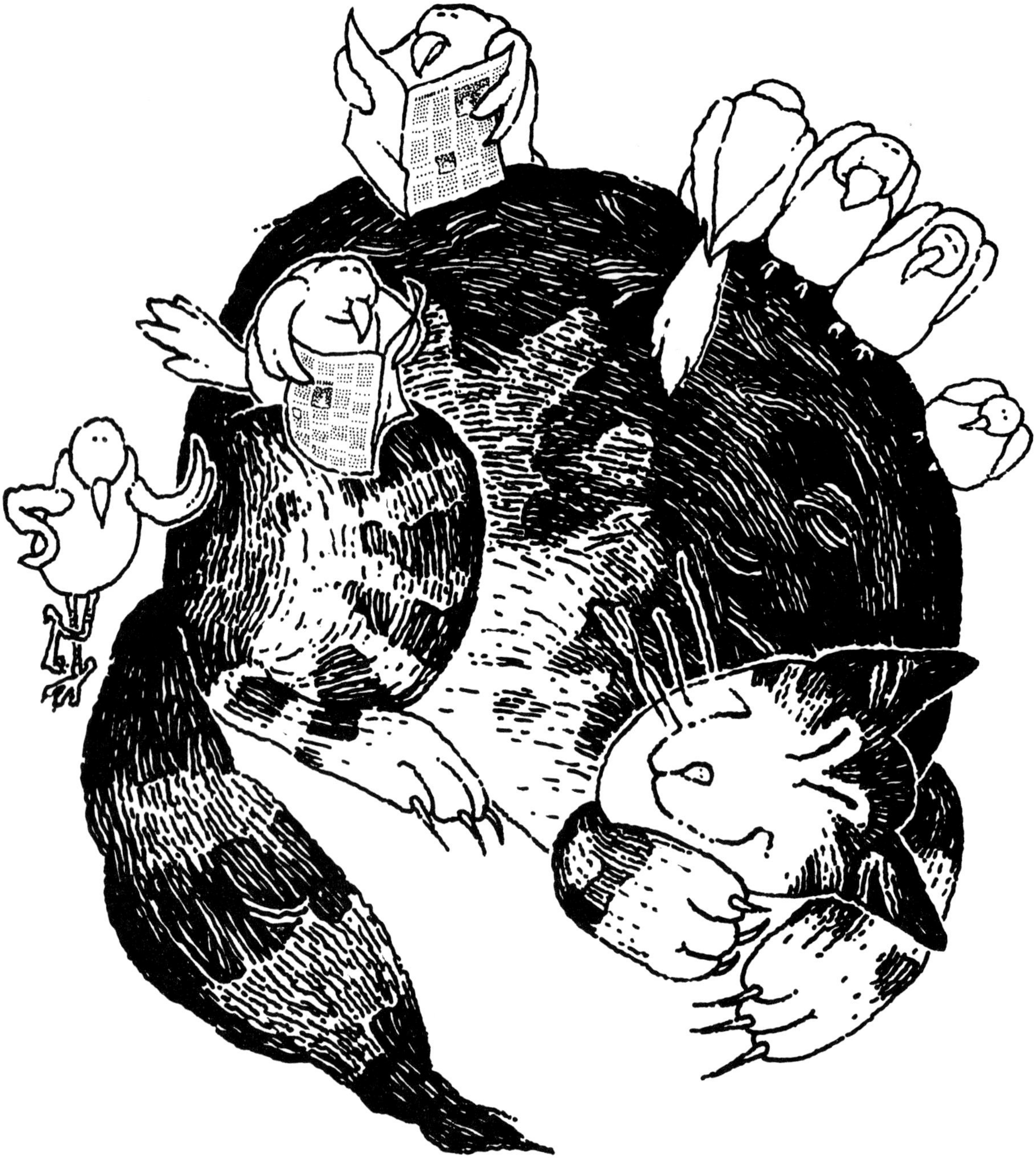

sLeePing Cat

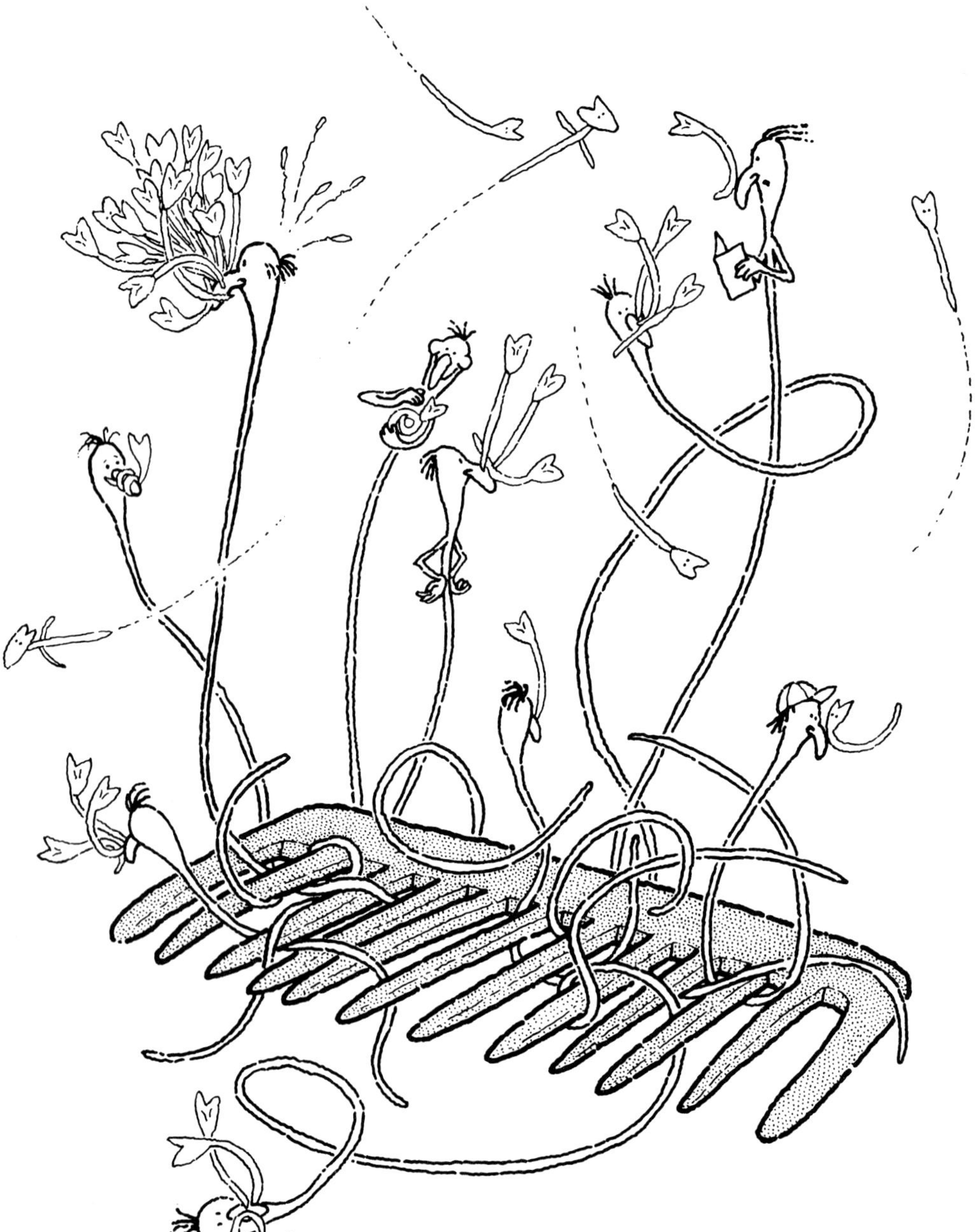

human hair meets cat hair

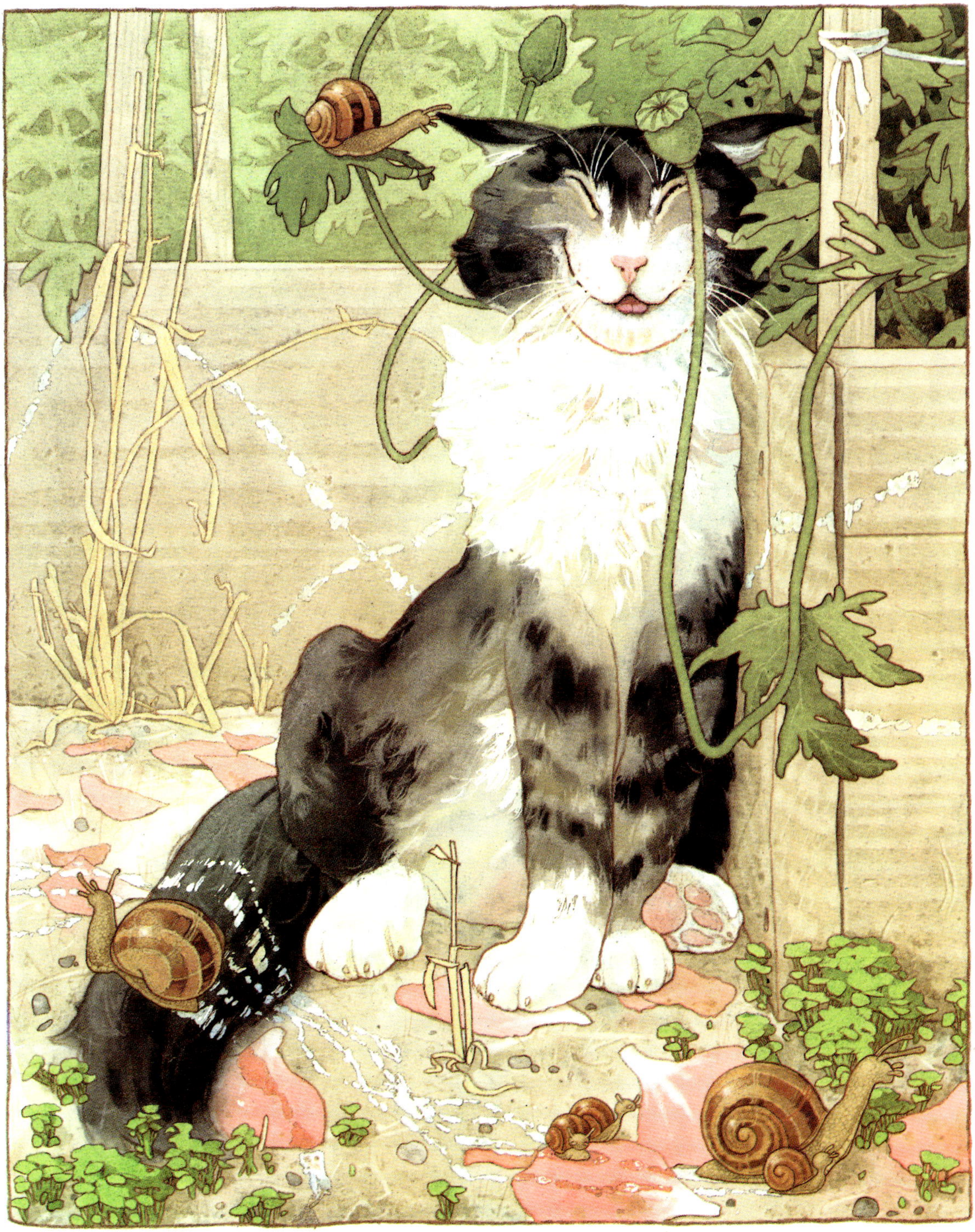

Sweetpea under the Poppies

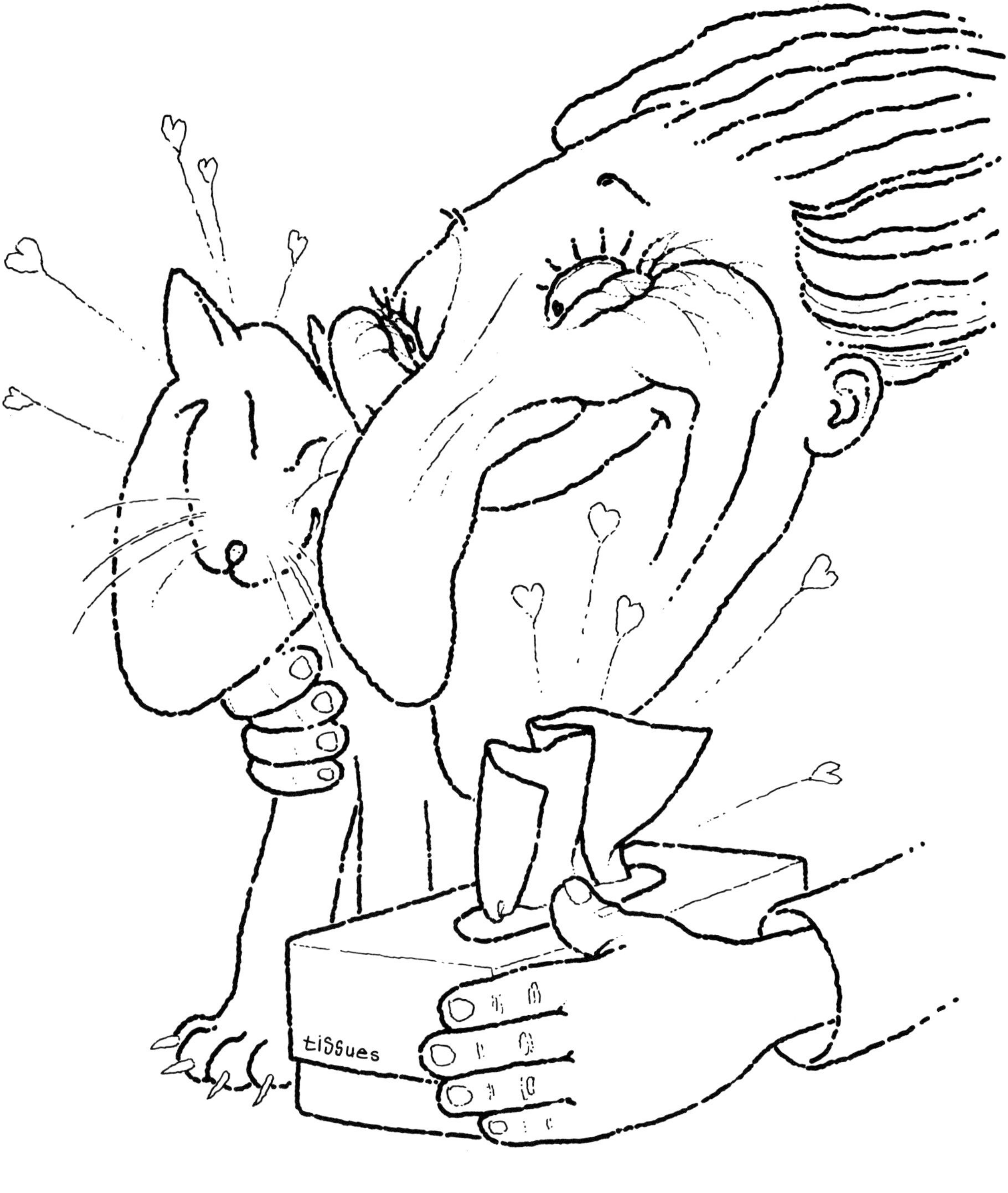
tissues

man's best friends

Lap Cat

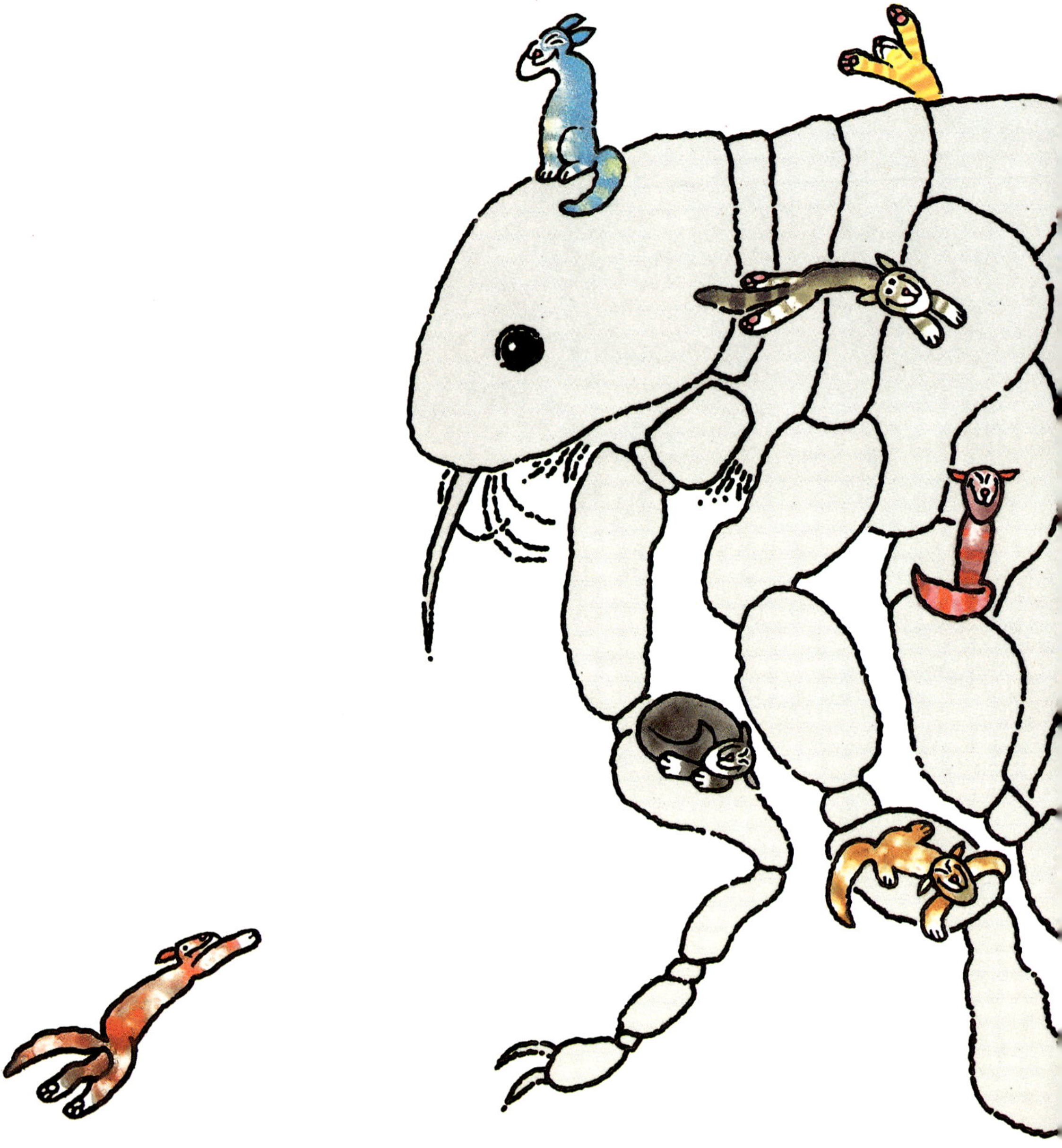

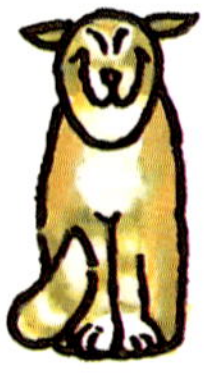

Little known fact

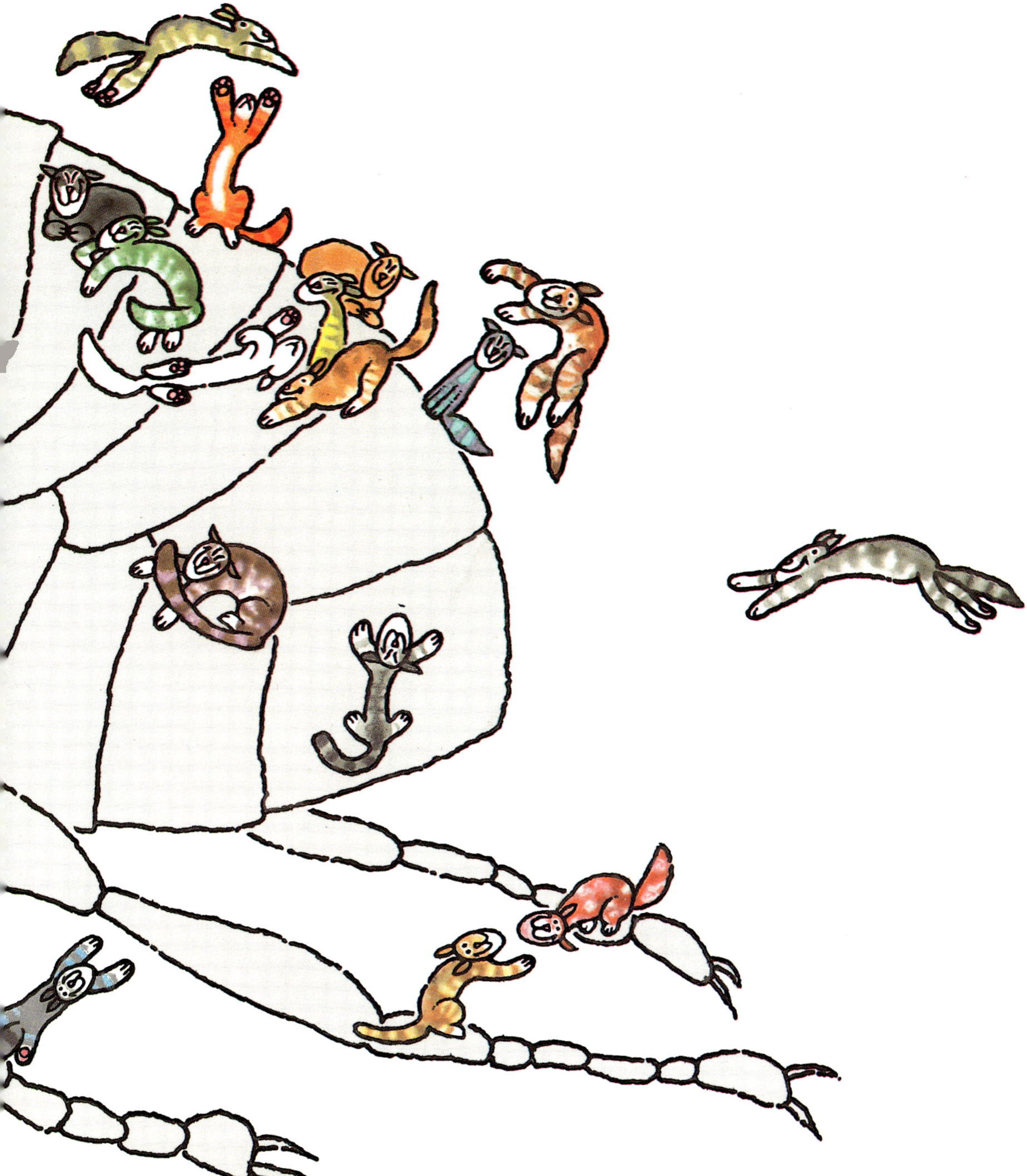

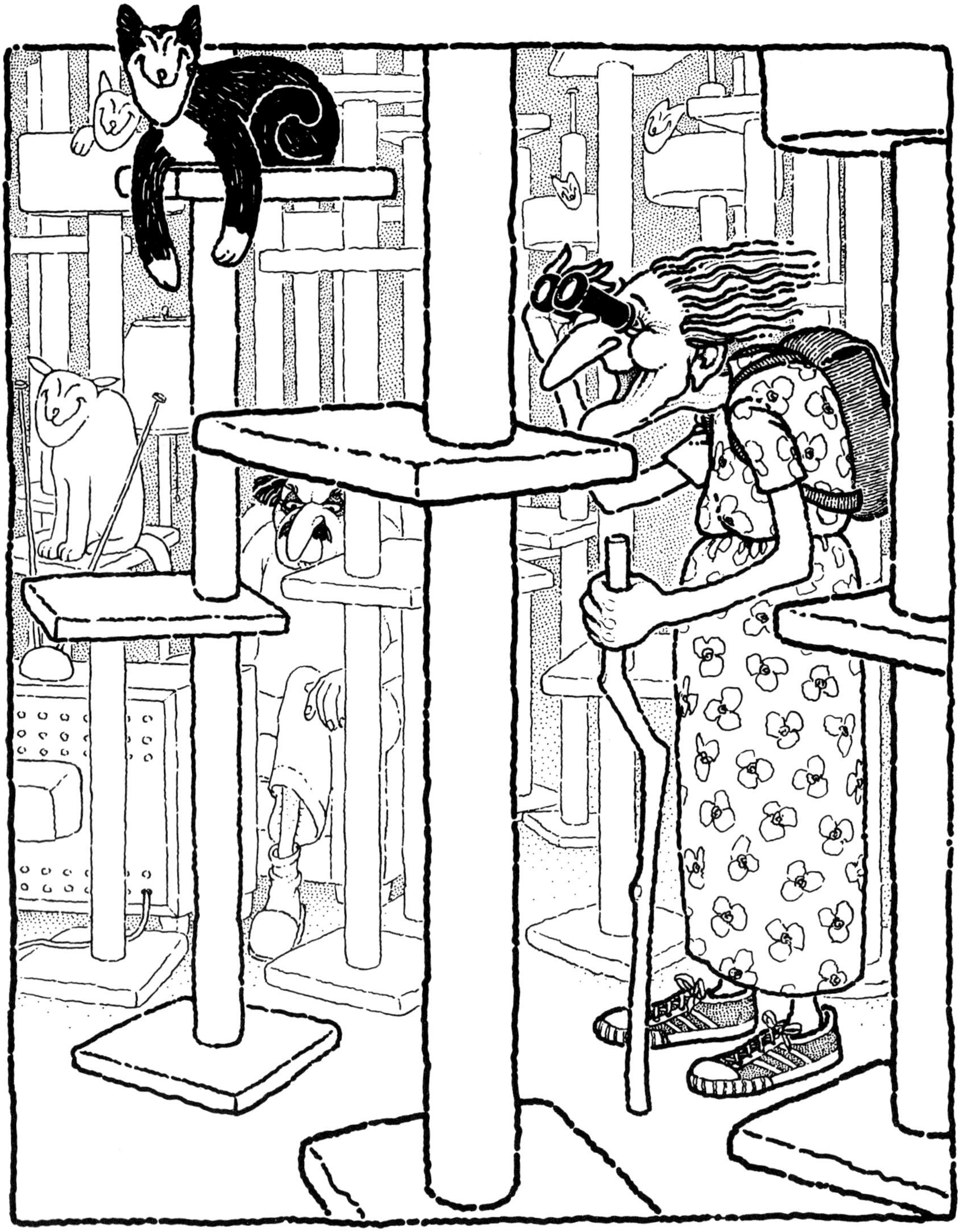

"oh look Neddy, it's a white-breasted flycatcher."

cat
overcome with
sadness on having just
recited a tragic
poem
in norwegian

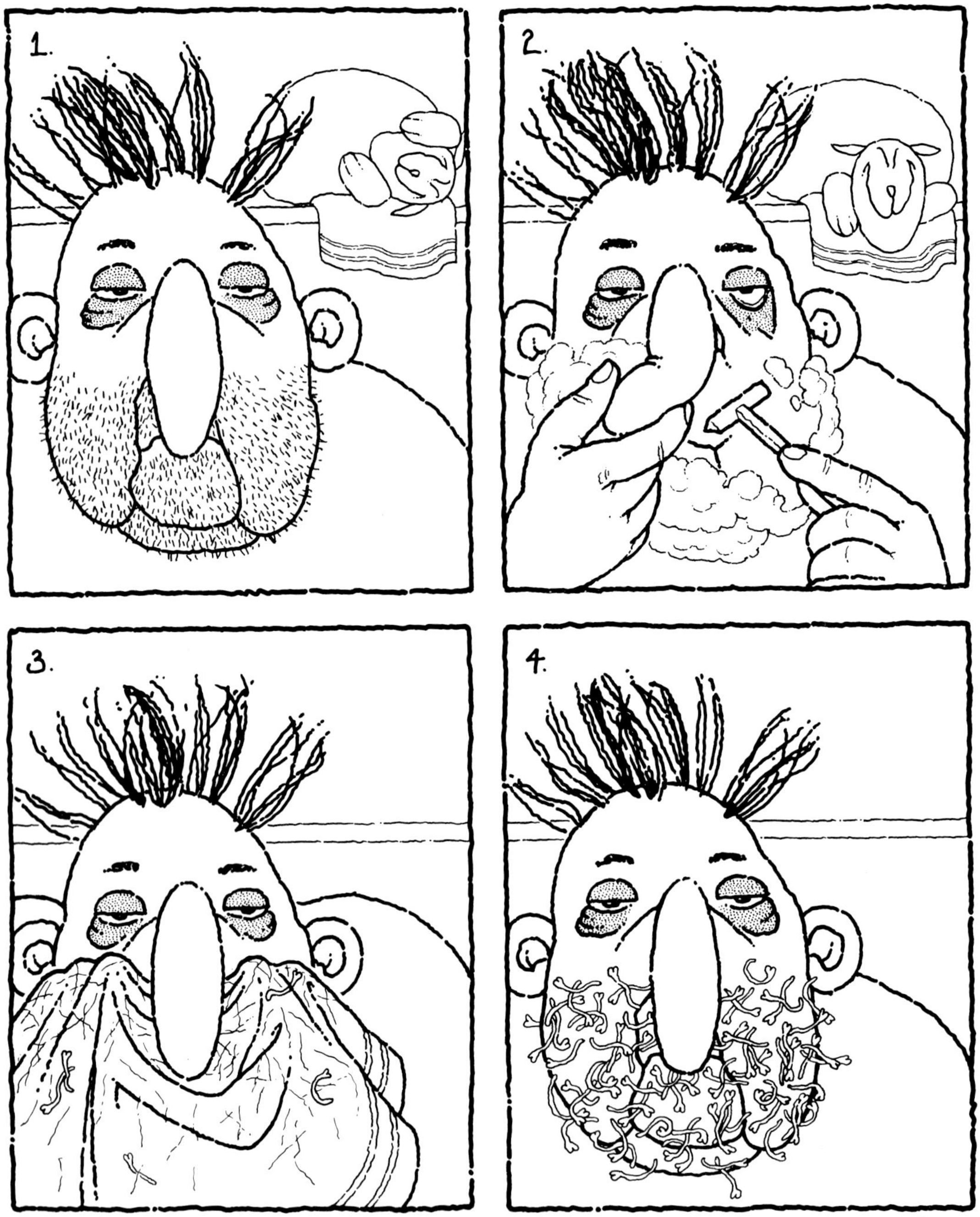
1.
2.
3.
4.

Morning Shave

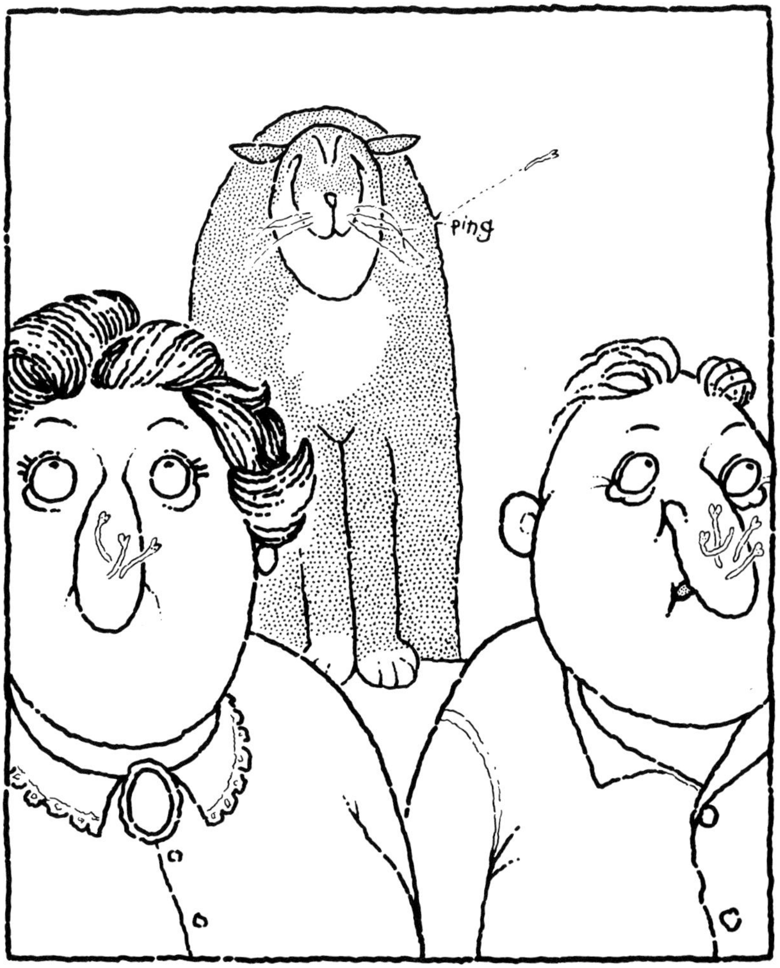
ping

for several years mr. and mrs. spittoon
have wondered about "ping"

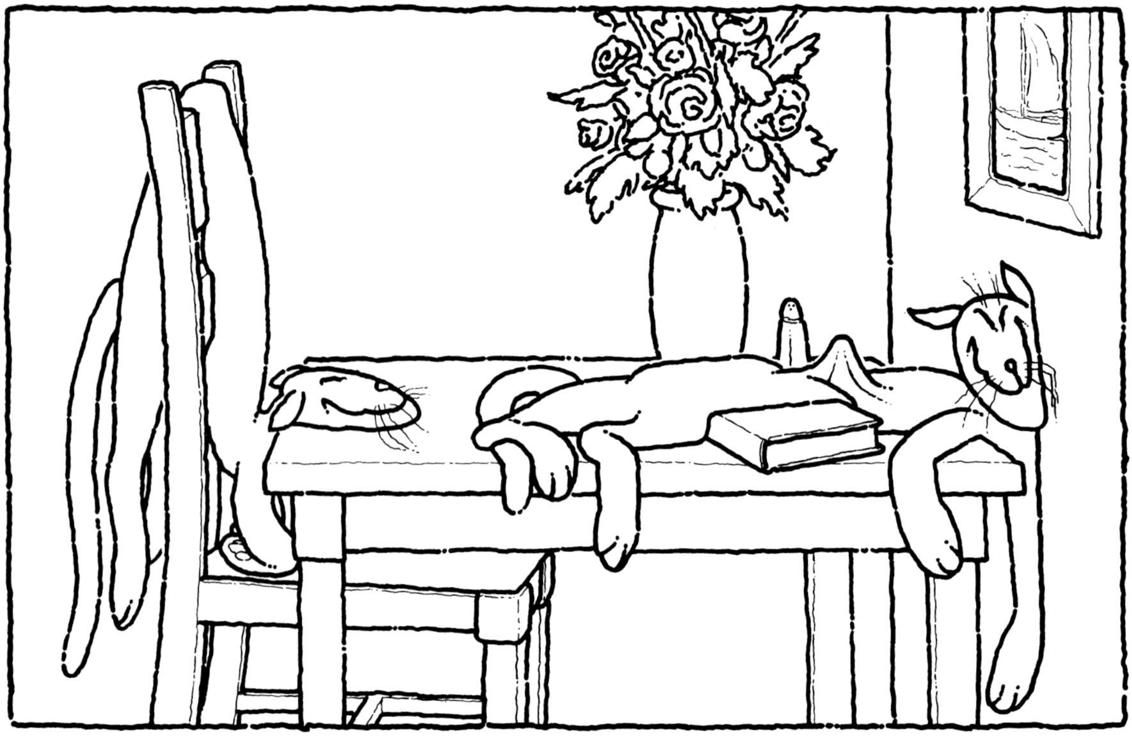

relaxed cats

allergic reaction to cats

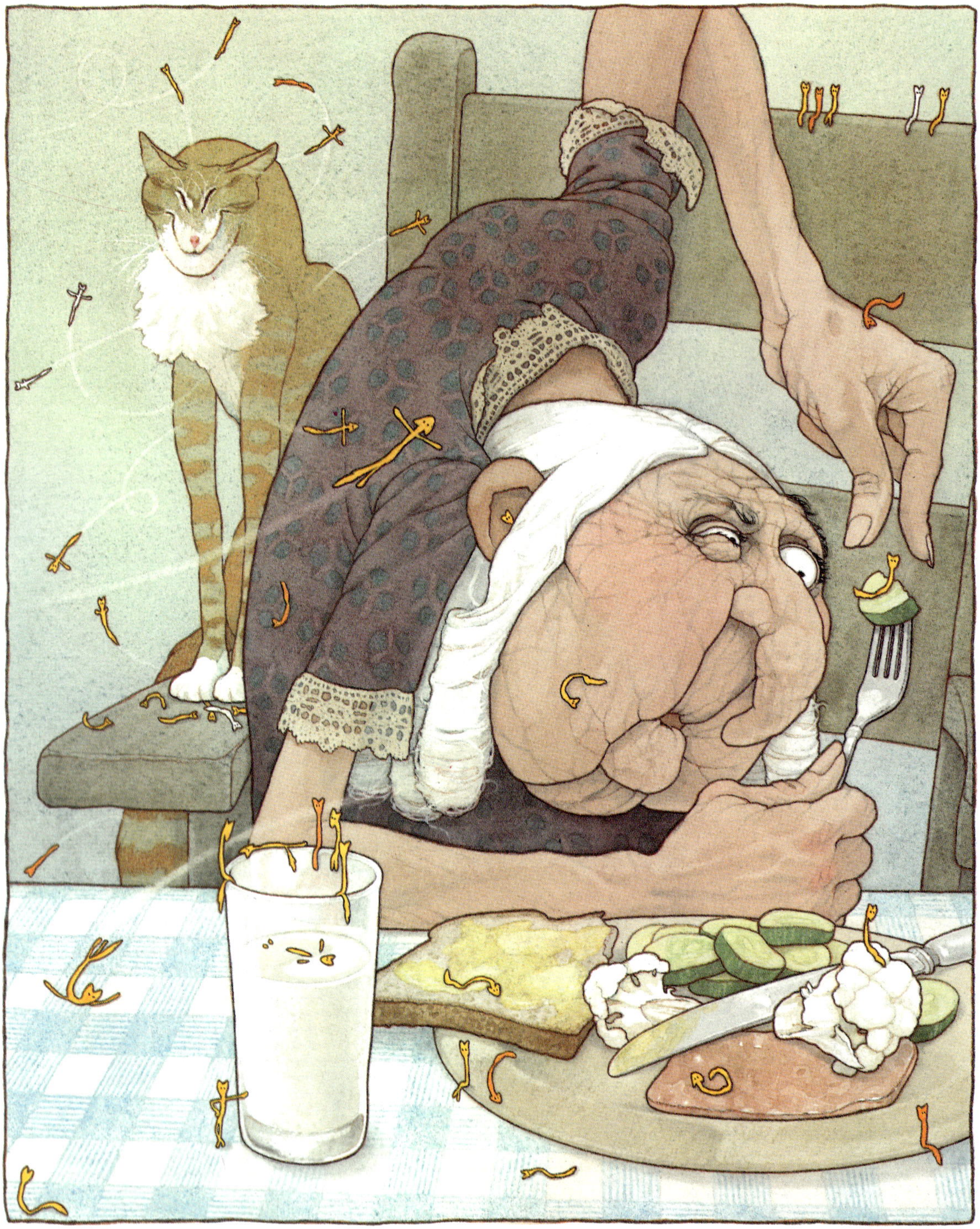

cat hair everywhere

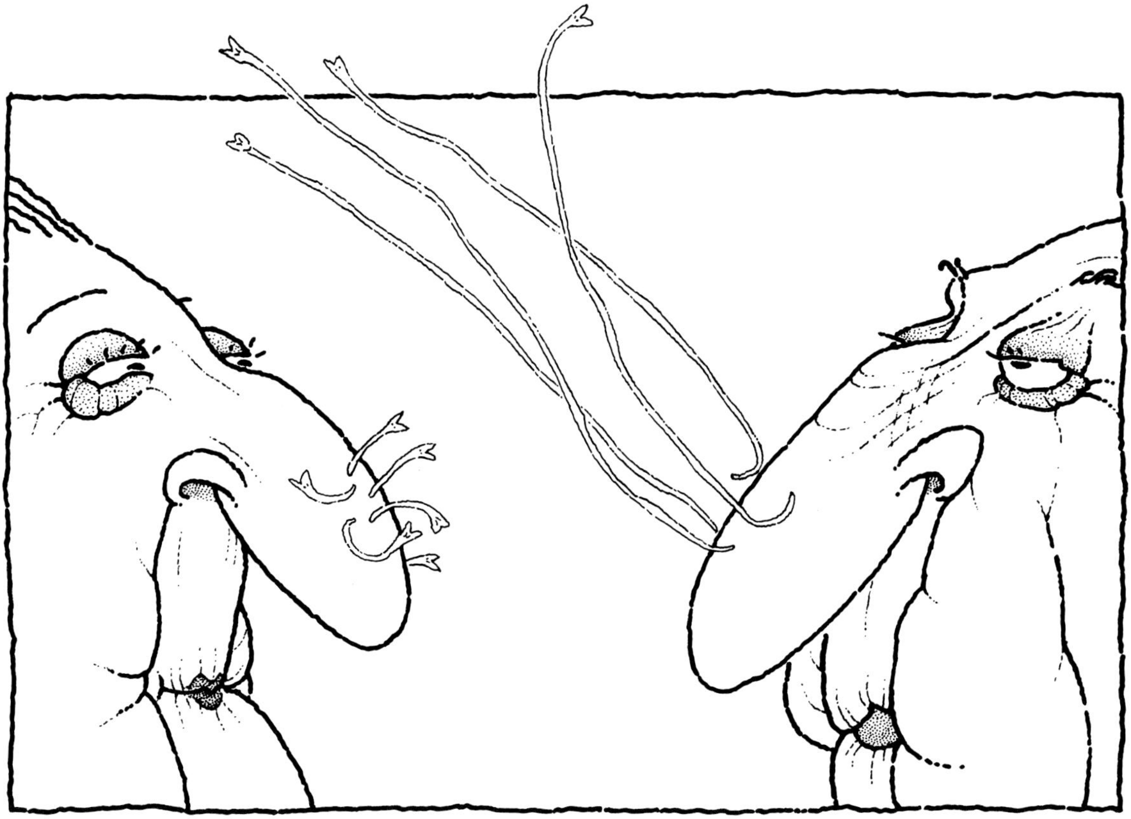

"...and what kind of cat do You have?" "Longhaired tabby".

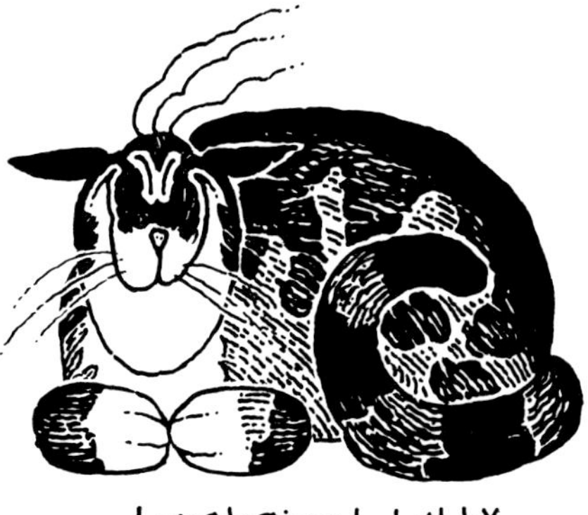

Longhaired tabby

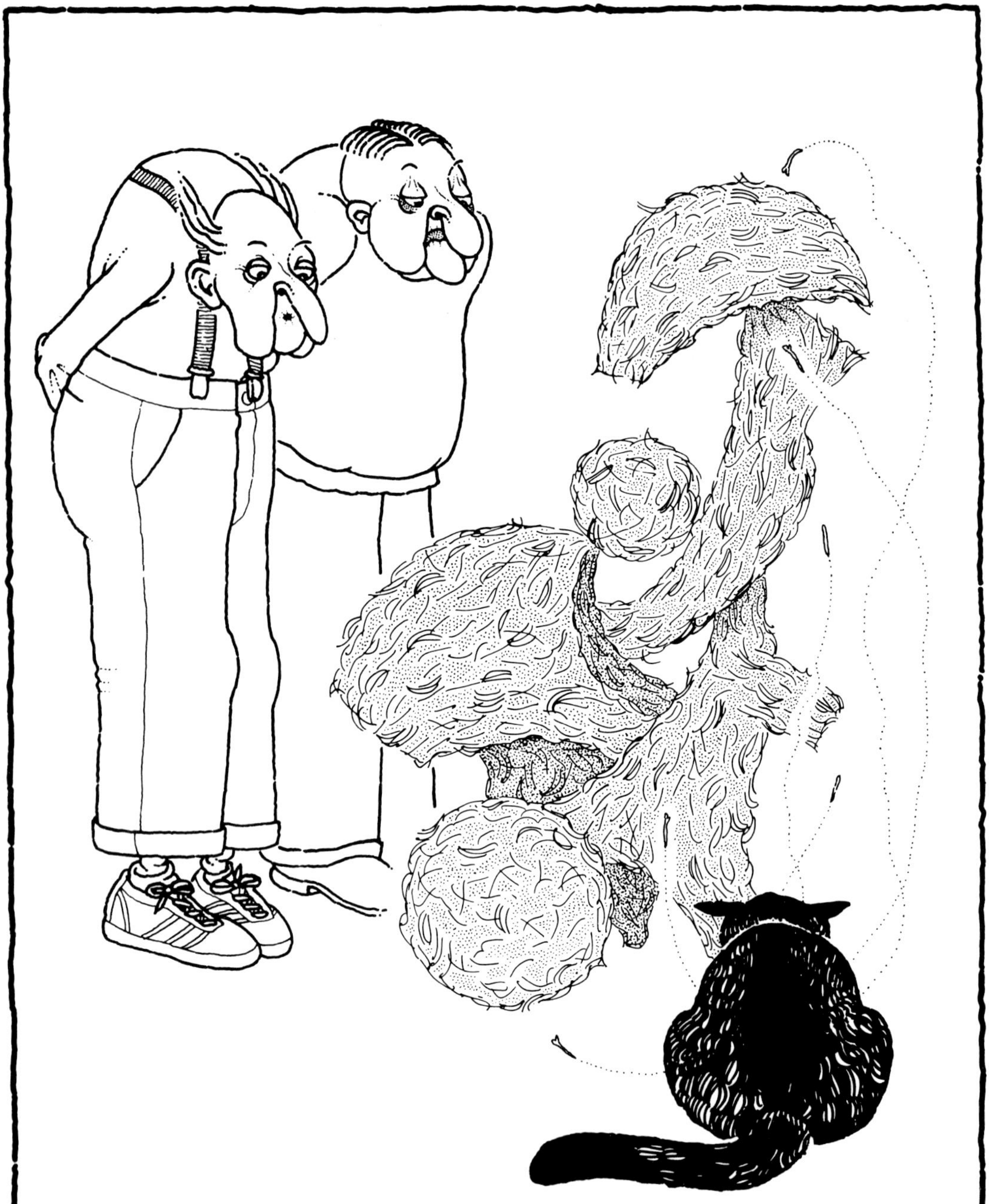

"it's just something the cat has been working on."

Are you embarrassed by birds sitting on your nose? Do cat hairs make you sneeze?

Then you need a NOZE·IT Scarecrow.
This adorable little scarecrow not only frightens away those pesky flying cat hairs, but it also keeps the crows off your nose too – a big plus!

Lonely? Shy at parties? New in town?
Become the most popular guy or gal around. Just slip a NOZE·IT Scarecrow Boy or Girl on your nose and become the center of attention.

Specify when ordering:
☐ SCARECROW BOY
☐ SCARECROW GIRL

Outfitters to noses since Moses.

NOZE·IT · Attn: Scarecrow Dept. · Cat Hair Rd. · Nose, CA 86222

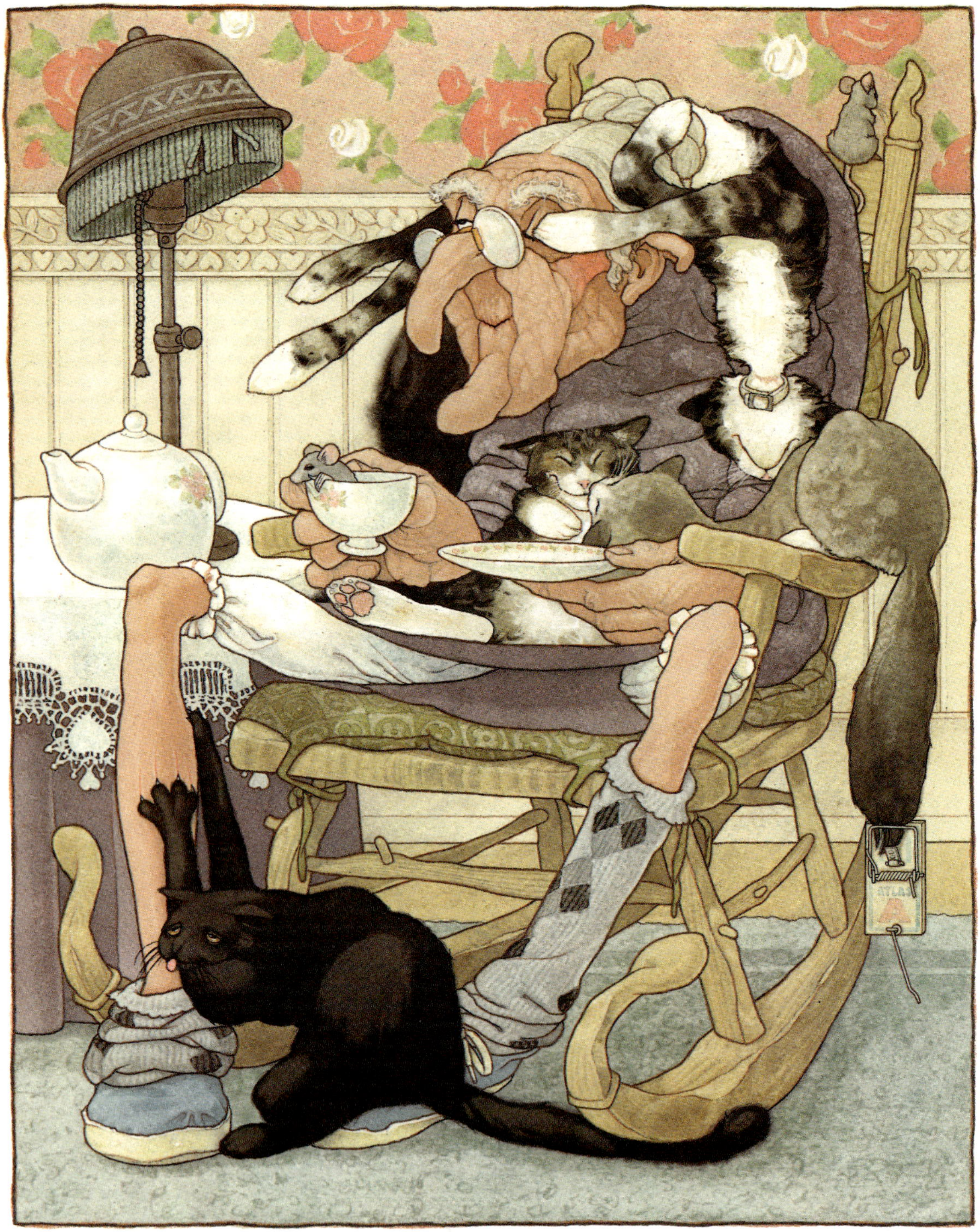
ATLAS
A

old Lady with Cats

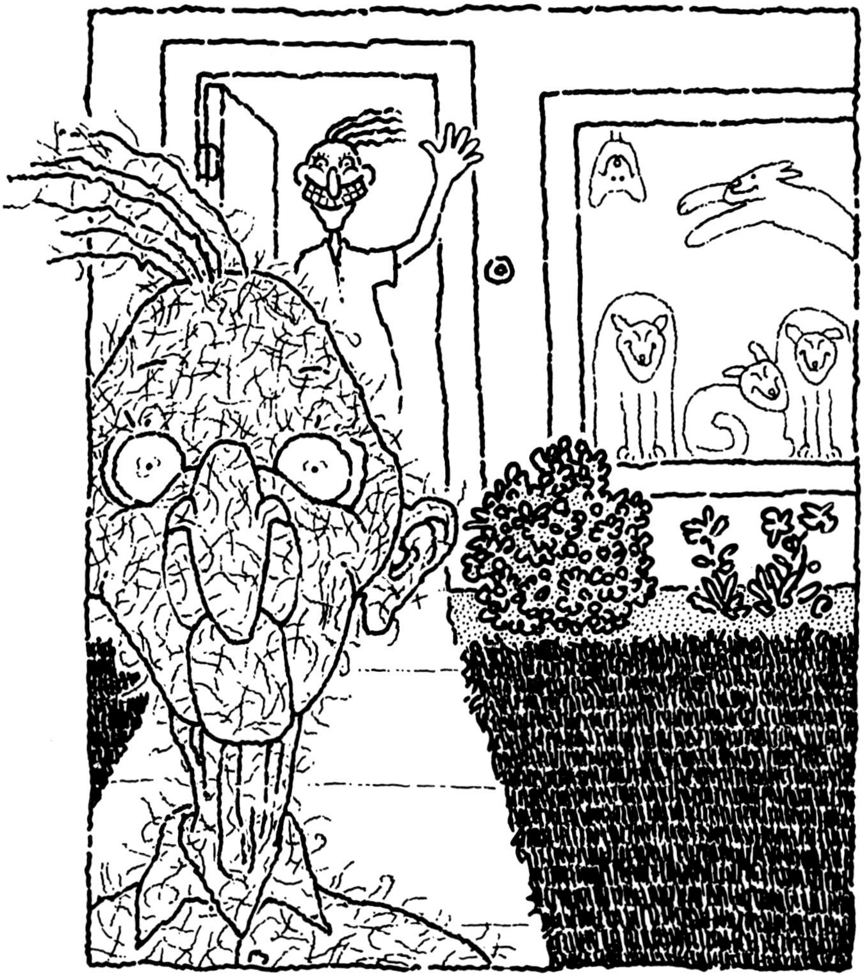

a visit to fred's house

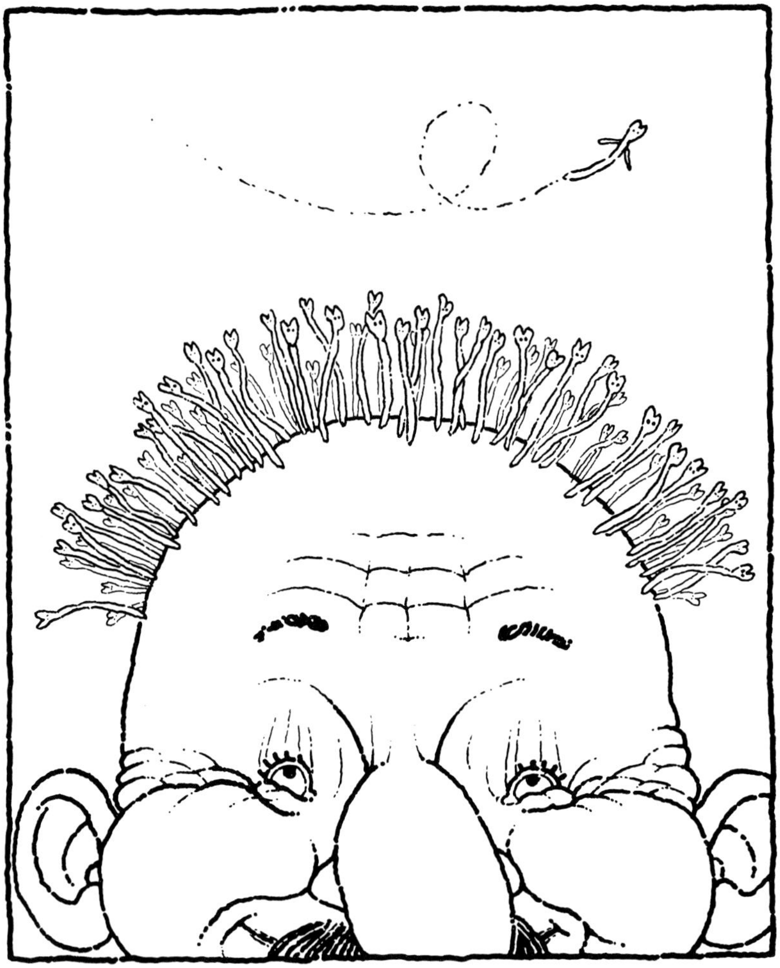

a happy bald man and trained cat hair

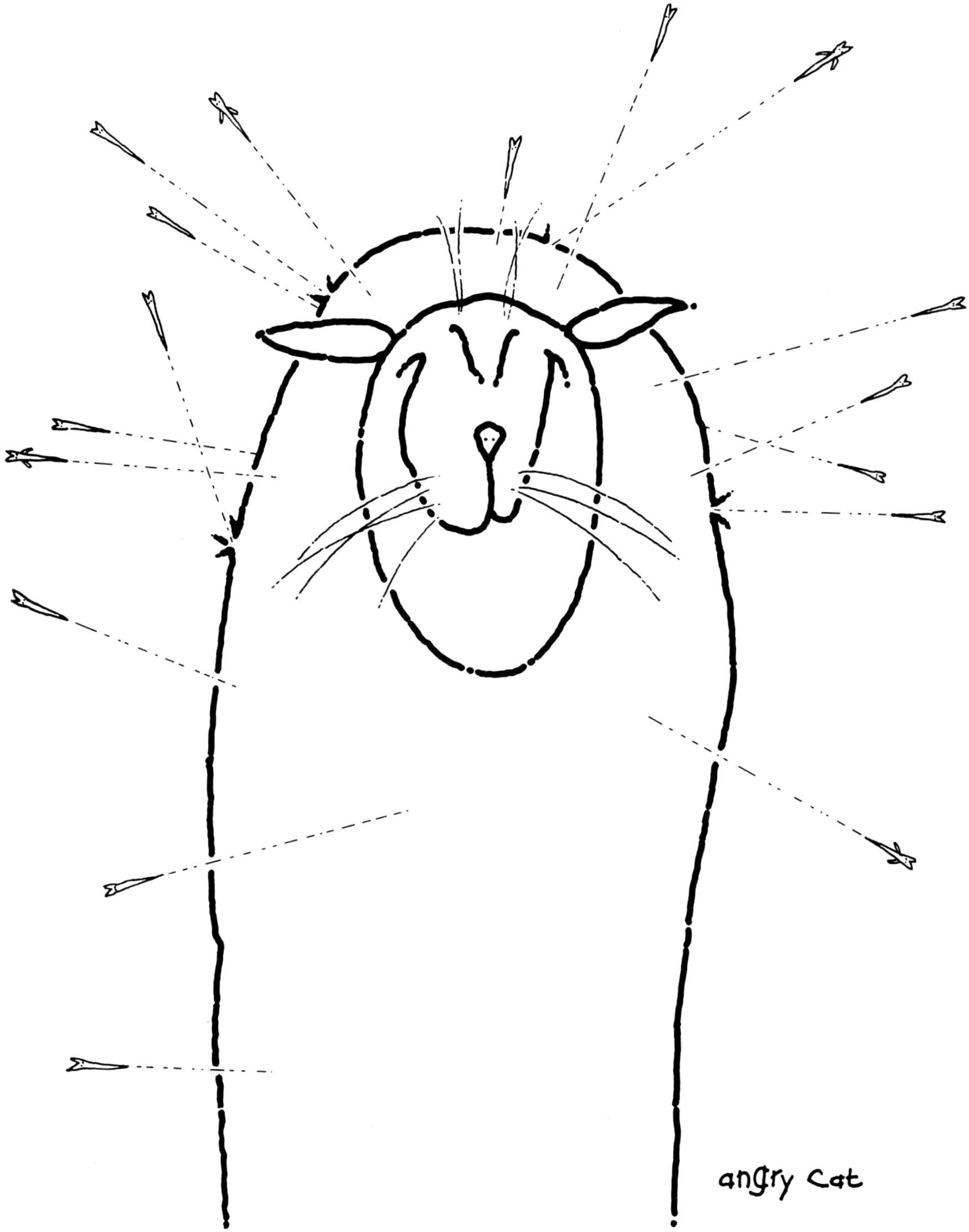

angry cat

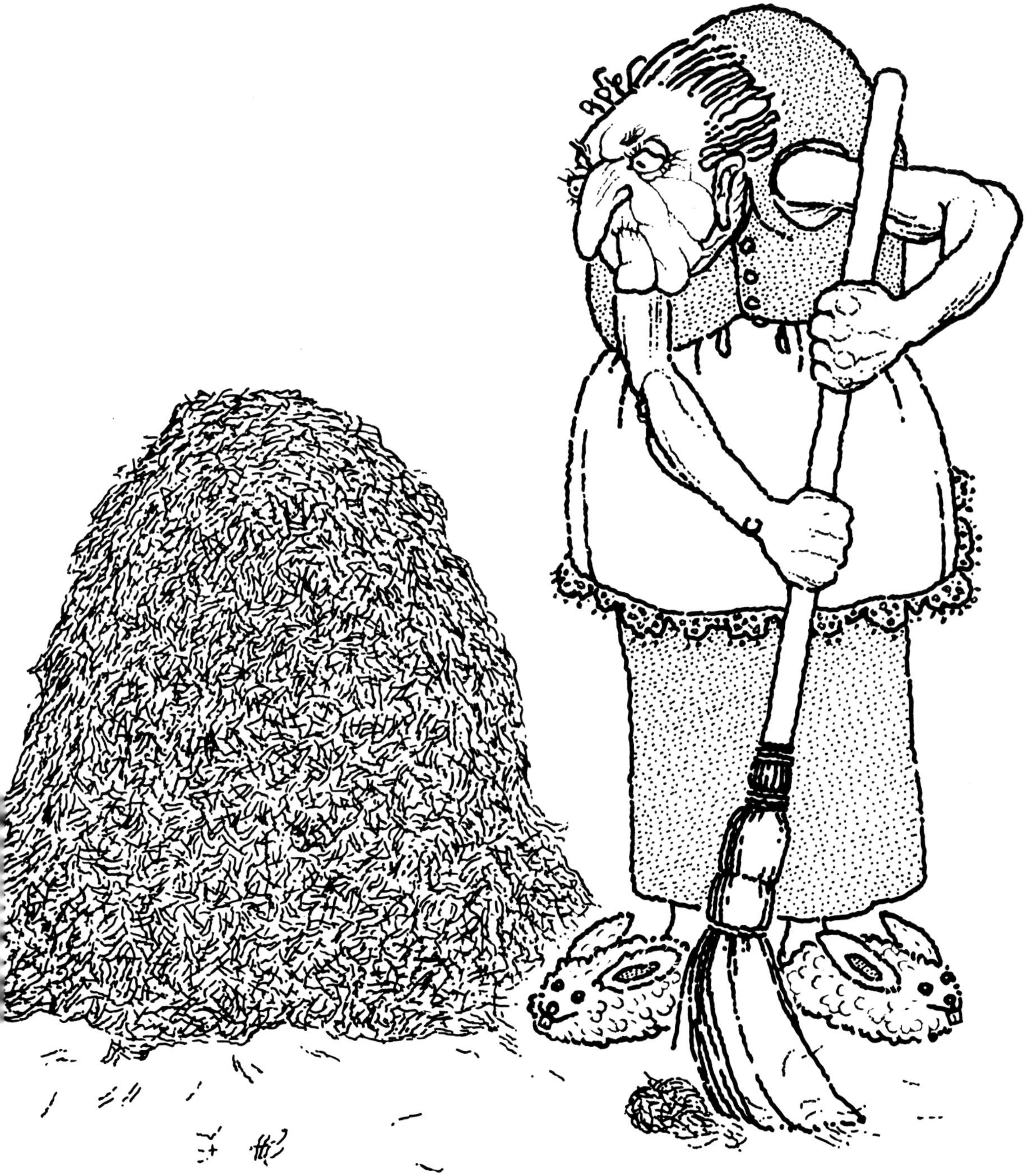

a Seed saga

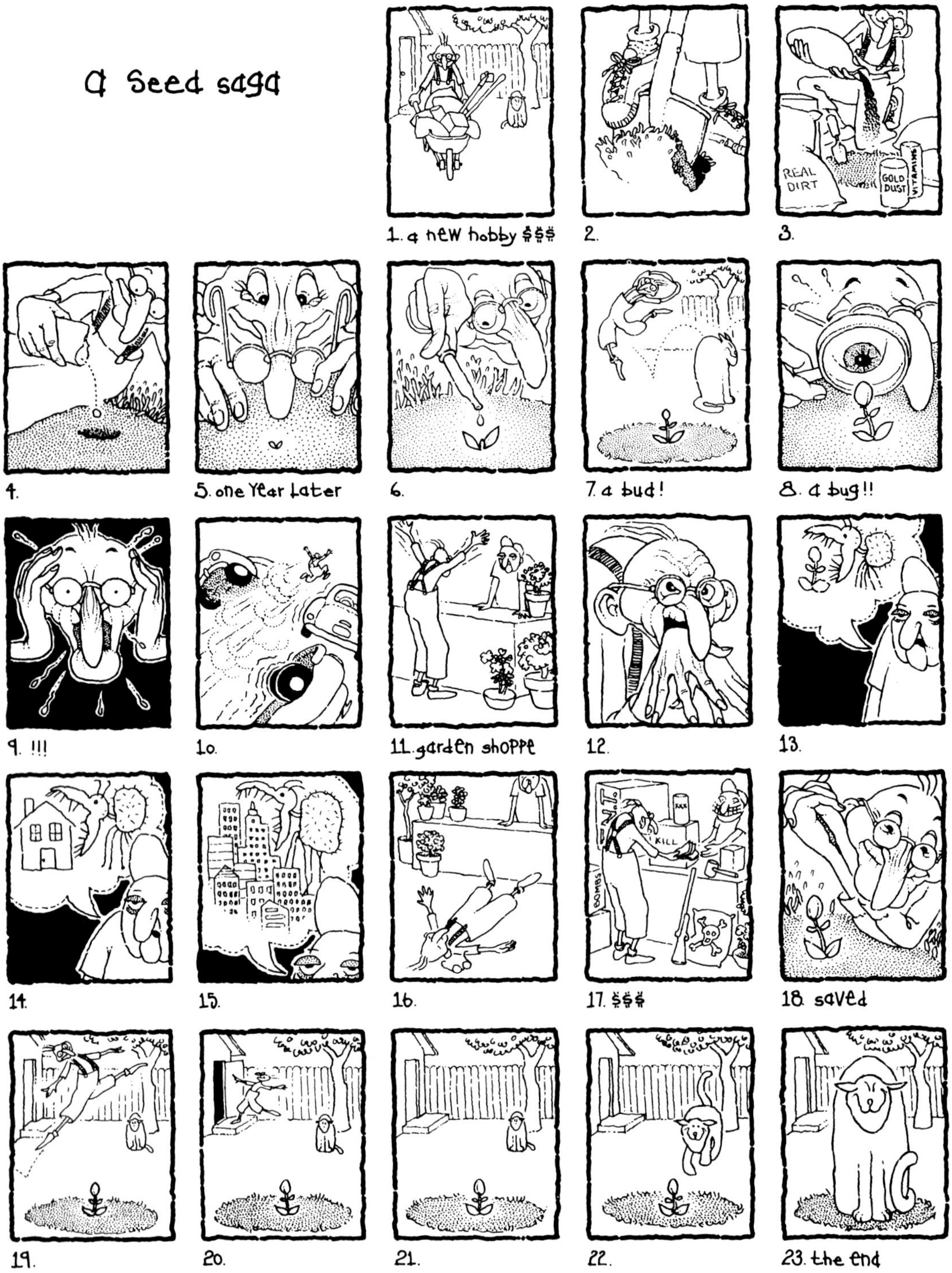
1. a new hobby $$$
2.
REAL DIRT
GOLD DUST
VITAMINS
3.
4.
5. one Year Later
6.
7. a bud!
8. a bug!!
9. !!!
10.
11. garden shoppe
12.
13.
14.
15.
16.
T.N.T.
XXX
KILL
BOMBS
17. $$$
18. saved
19.
20.
21.
22.
23. the end

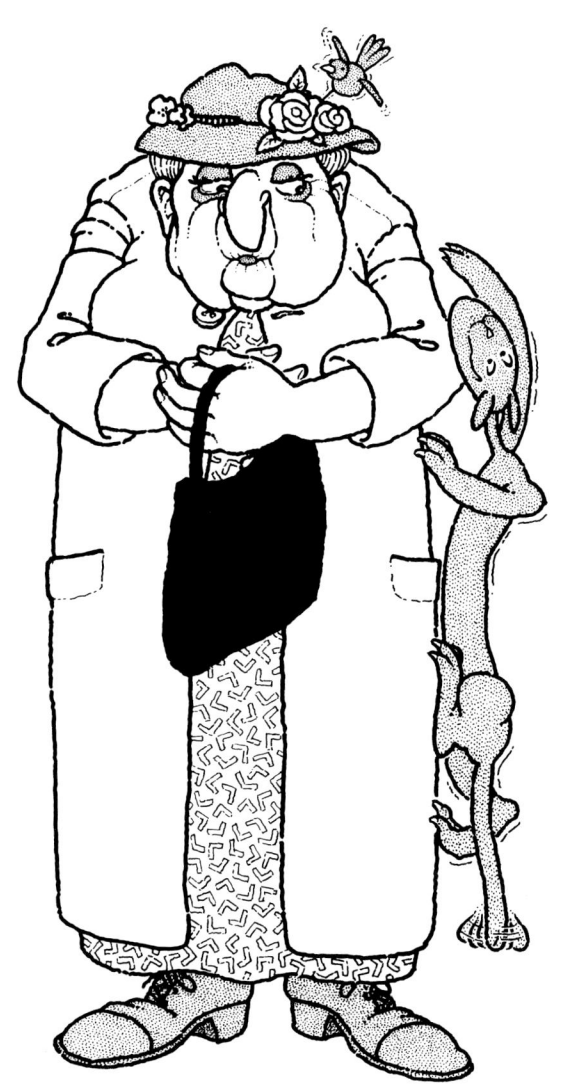

it's everywhere!

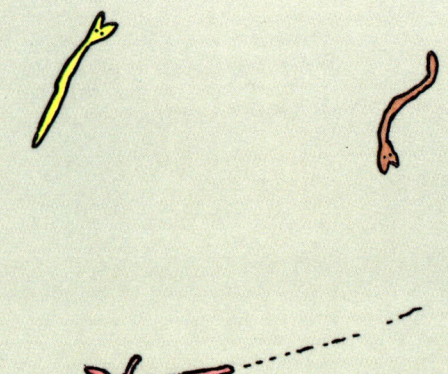

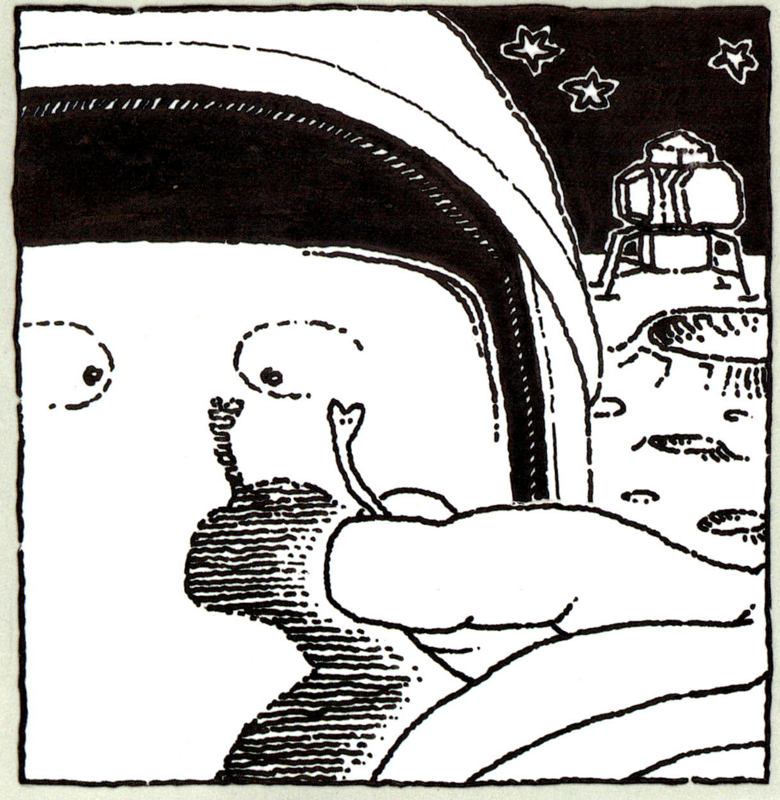

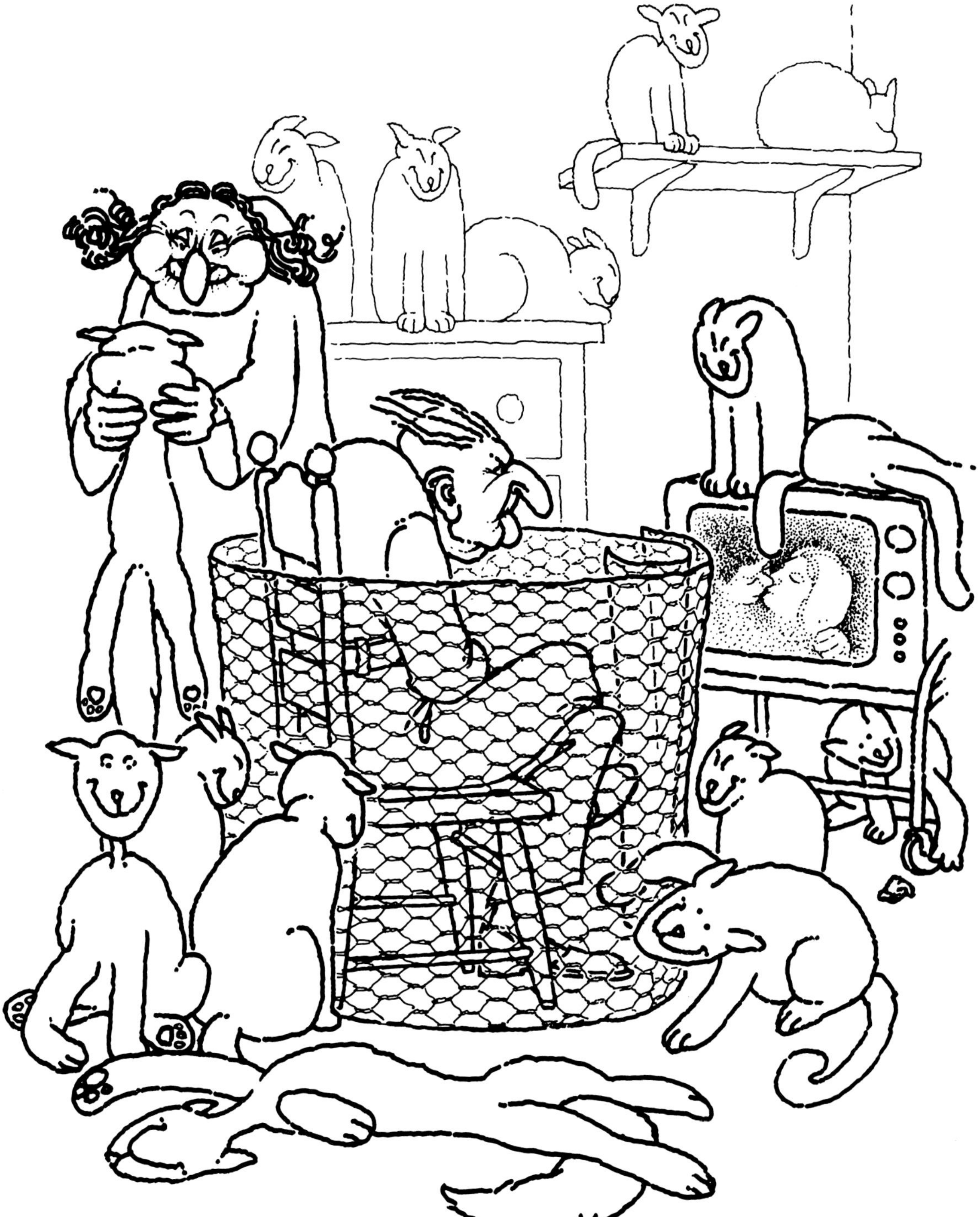

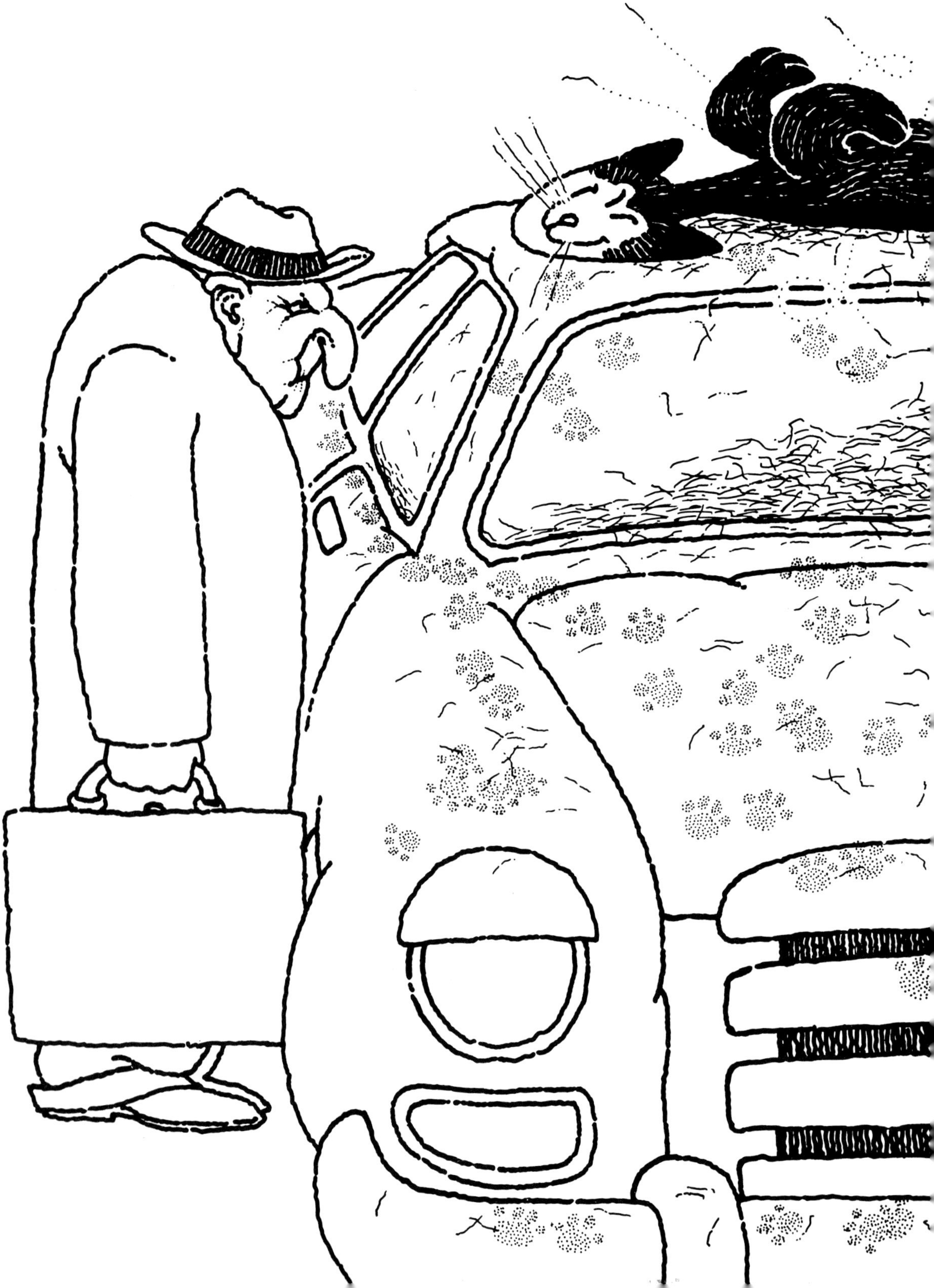

1.

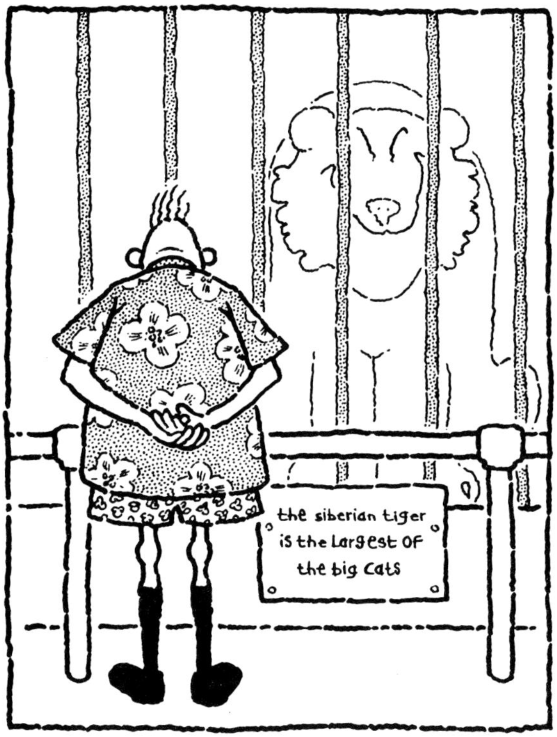
the siberian tiger
is the Largest of
the big Cats

2.

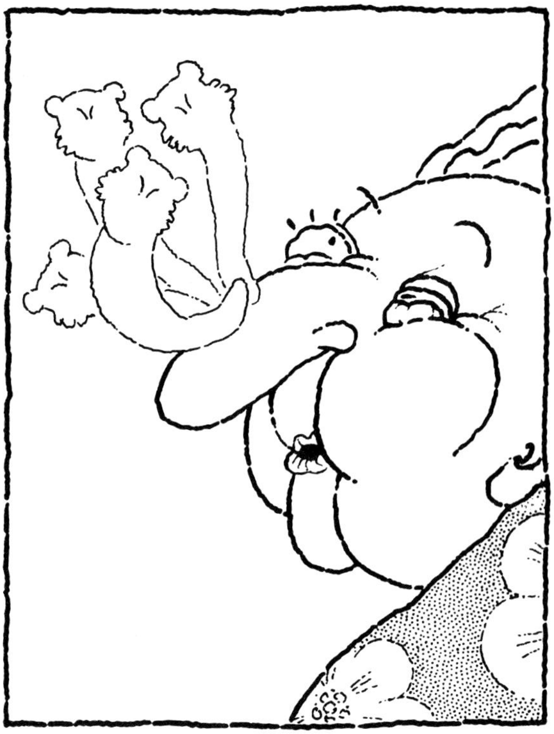

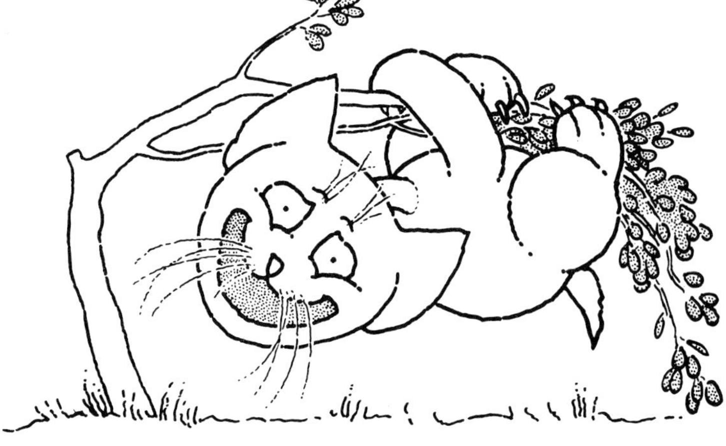

how to take a cat nap

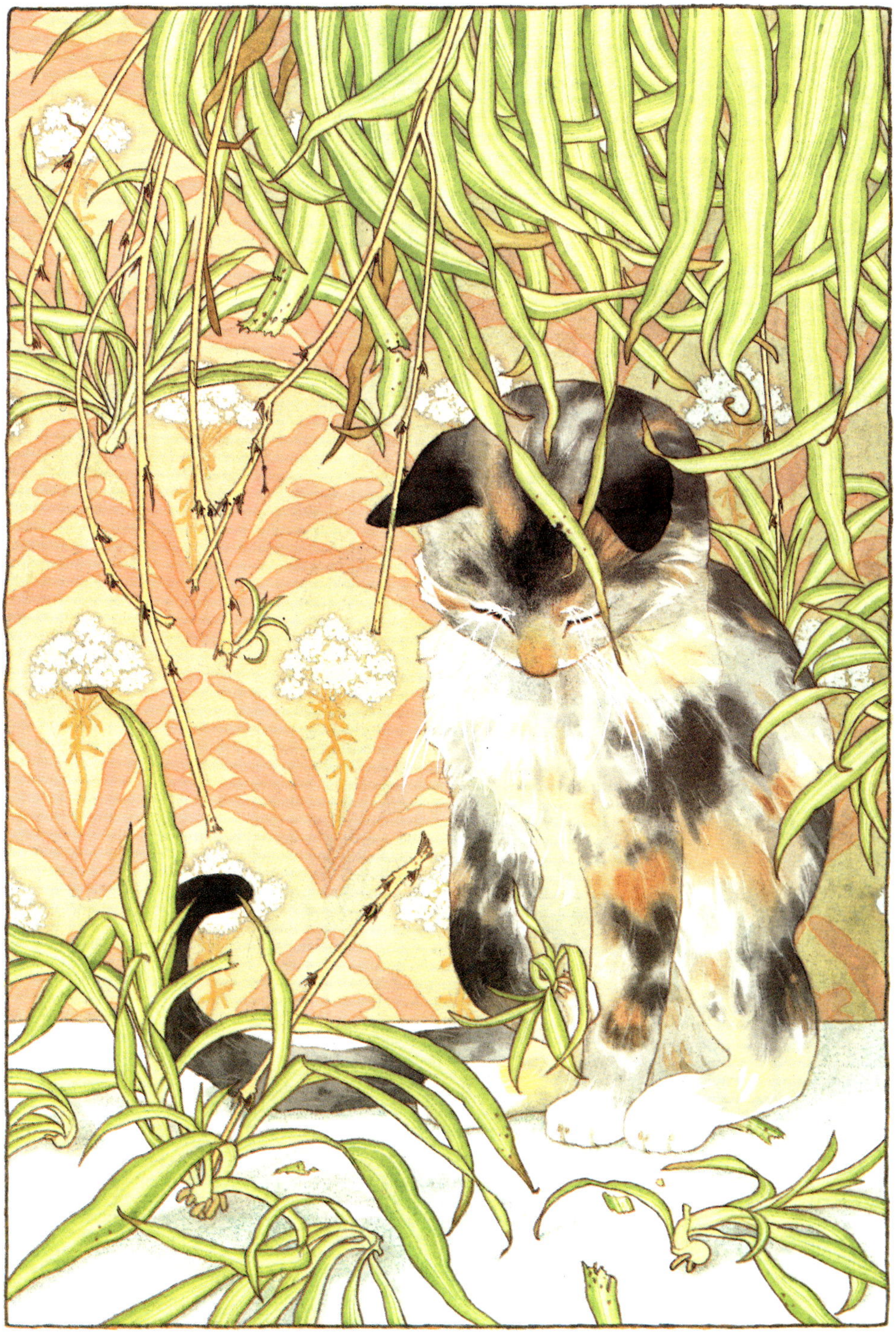

Professor Beans enjoys a Spider Plant

Cuteness kills!!!

Sneezing?
Has cat hair got you by the nose?

Then meet Spot.

This cute little angry sitting dog is a long-time NOZE·IT favorite. Spot is guaranteed to keep the cat hairs off your nose, and to put a smile on your face. You might say it's just what the 'dogtor' ordered for those pesky cat hairs.

Meet our newest NOZE•IT creation

FIERCE STANDING SPOT

Please specify when ordering:
- ☐ ANGRY SITTING SPOT
- ☐ FIERCE STANDING SPOT

Put a Spot on your nose today.
NOZE•IT · Attn: Spot Dept. · Cat Hair Rd. · Nose, CA 86222

NOZE·IT

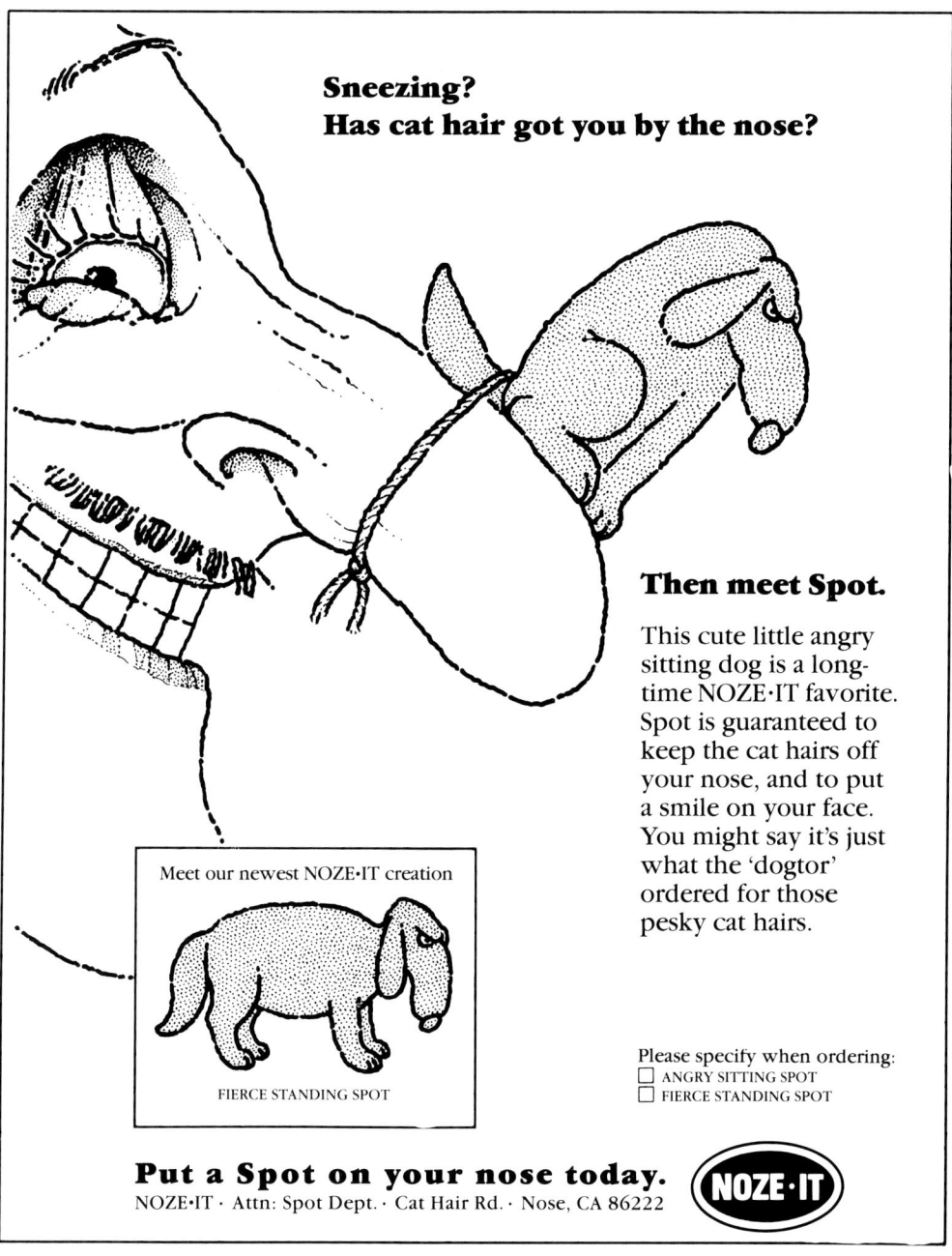

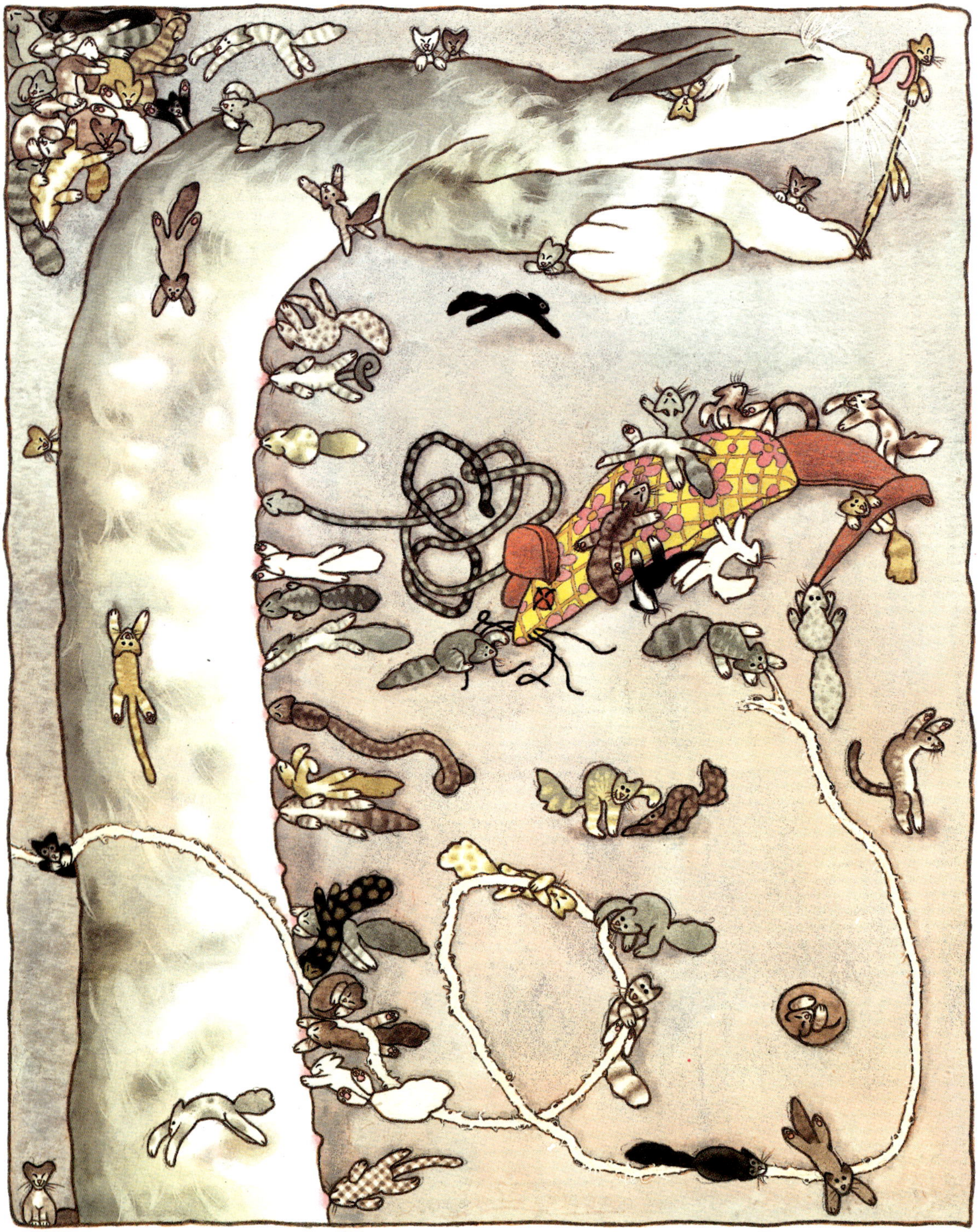

big litter

"...and so blah blah...my dog is so funny...and blah blah blah...i swear that dog actually laughs. Cats just don't have a sense of humor."

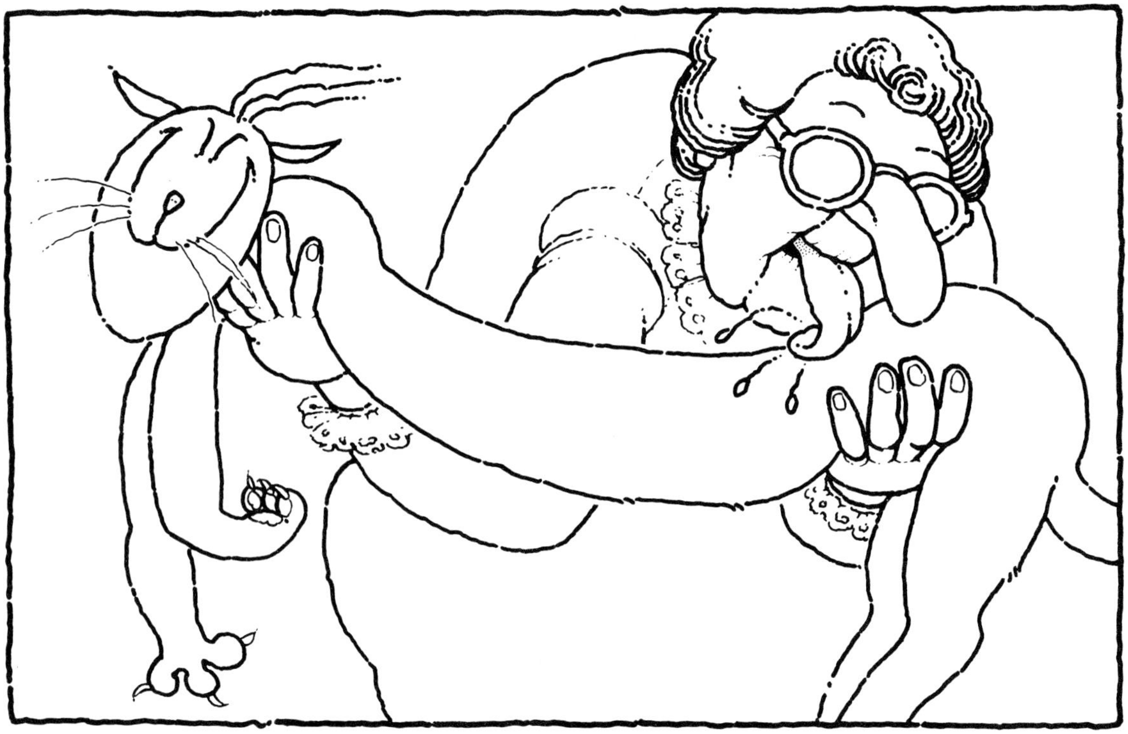

Lucille gives iddie Biddie a bath

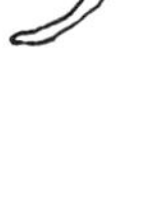

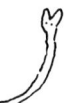

HOW TO BE YOUR CAT'S BEST FRIEND, YOU MUSCLEHEAD! 101

Do you bark when you beckon? Do you grunt a lot? Are you a 300 pound sewermouthed Hell's Angel with large pores? Are you covered with coarse hairs and manly mustaches, manly scars, and manly tattoos—and stink? CAN YOU READ THIS?

If the answer to any of these questions is "Yes," and you are seeking a better relationship with your cat, then this course is designed for you. We will explore the cat hidden within you.

- Learn simple effeminate gestures your cat will flip over.
- Polish your pidgin English.
- Learn how to find your high tiny voice.
- Learn how to break the ice with catnip and armpit odor aphrodisiacs.
- Learn how to play Mousie, Who's Got a Tickly Tummy?, and Fingers On Parade Past the Big Naughty Kitty Hiding Inside the Brown Paper Bag.

Instructor: Ms. Winnie Tittums
MWF 7 P.M., Room 112, Founder's Hall
2 Units, Credit/Non-Credit

DAH! KUTE F__KIN' KAT
HAR HAR

before taking ms. tittums class

DOE! issum a Keoot widow puddee? eeez Soo Keeoot!
hee hee hee

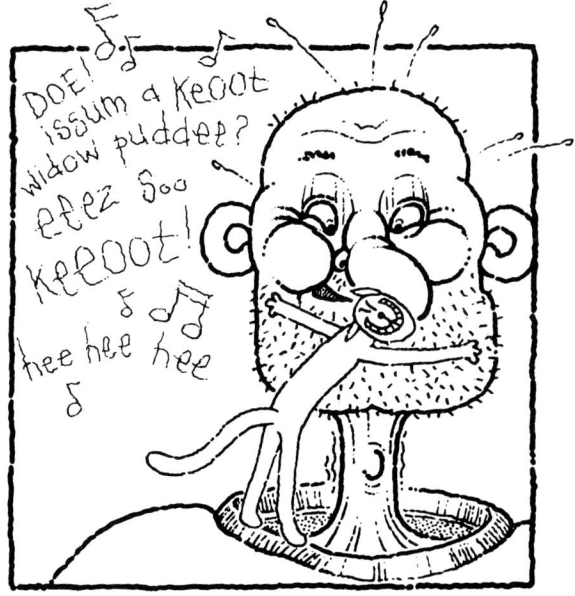

after taking ms. tittums class

cat
bristling
horribly with unbridled
anger over an
earlier encounter
with Wiener,
the illiterate dachshund,
whom,
inexplicably, slighted
him meanly

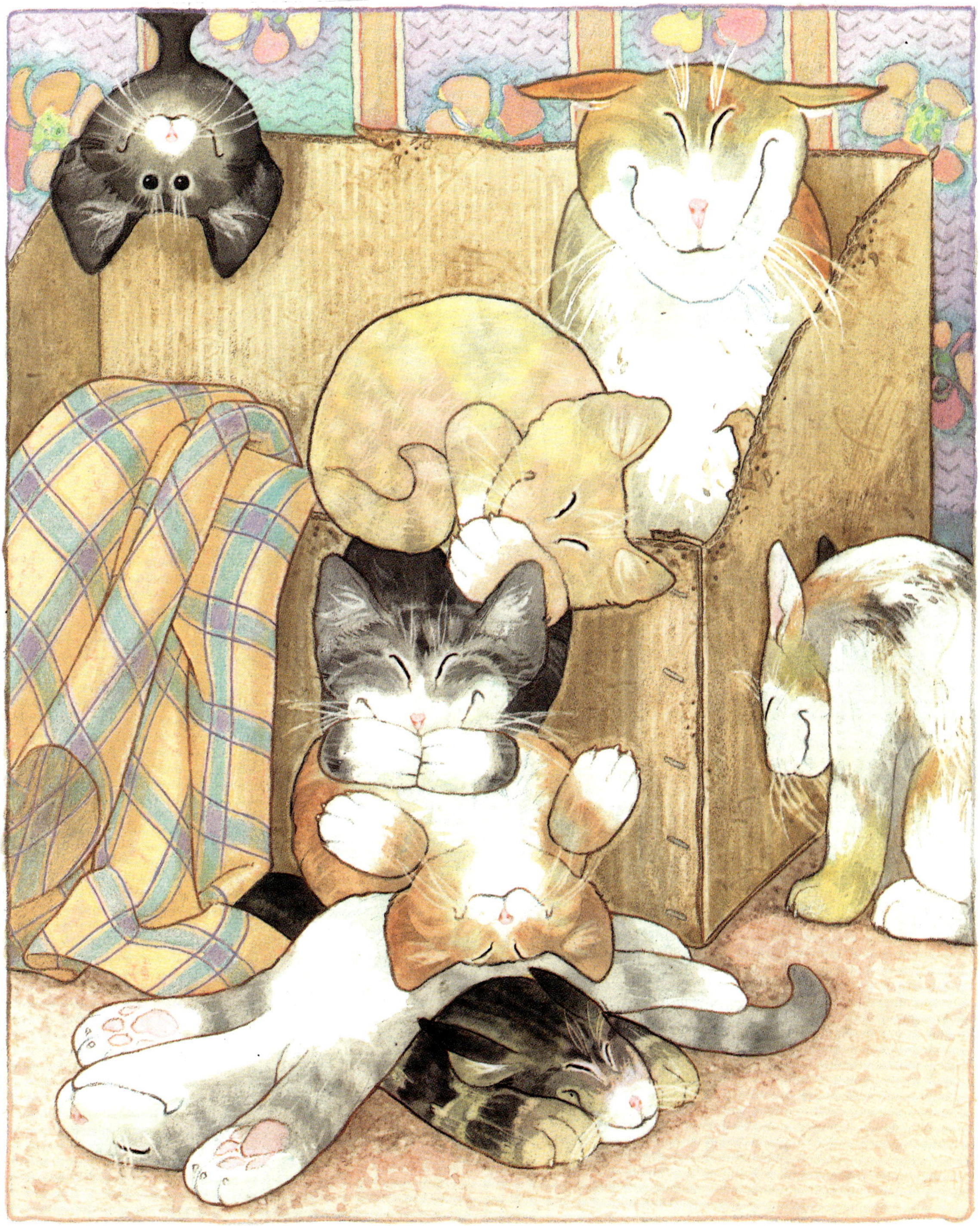

Nap time

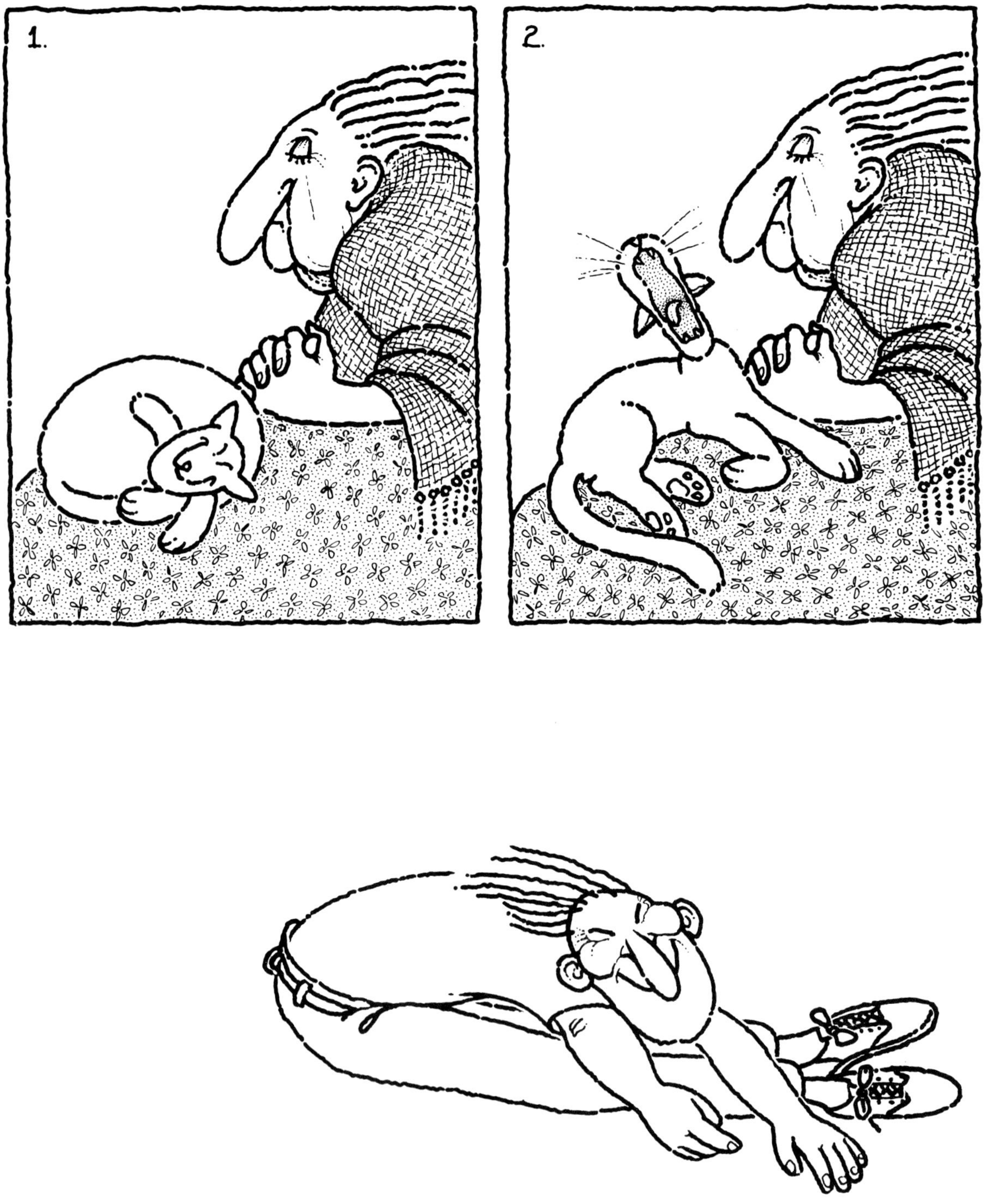
1.
2.

3.

Catnapping

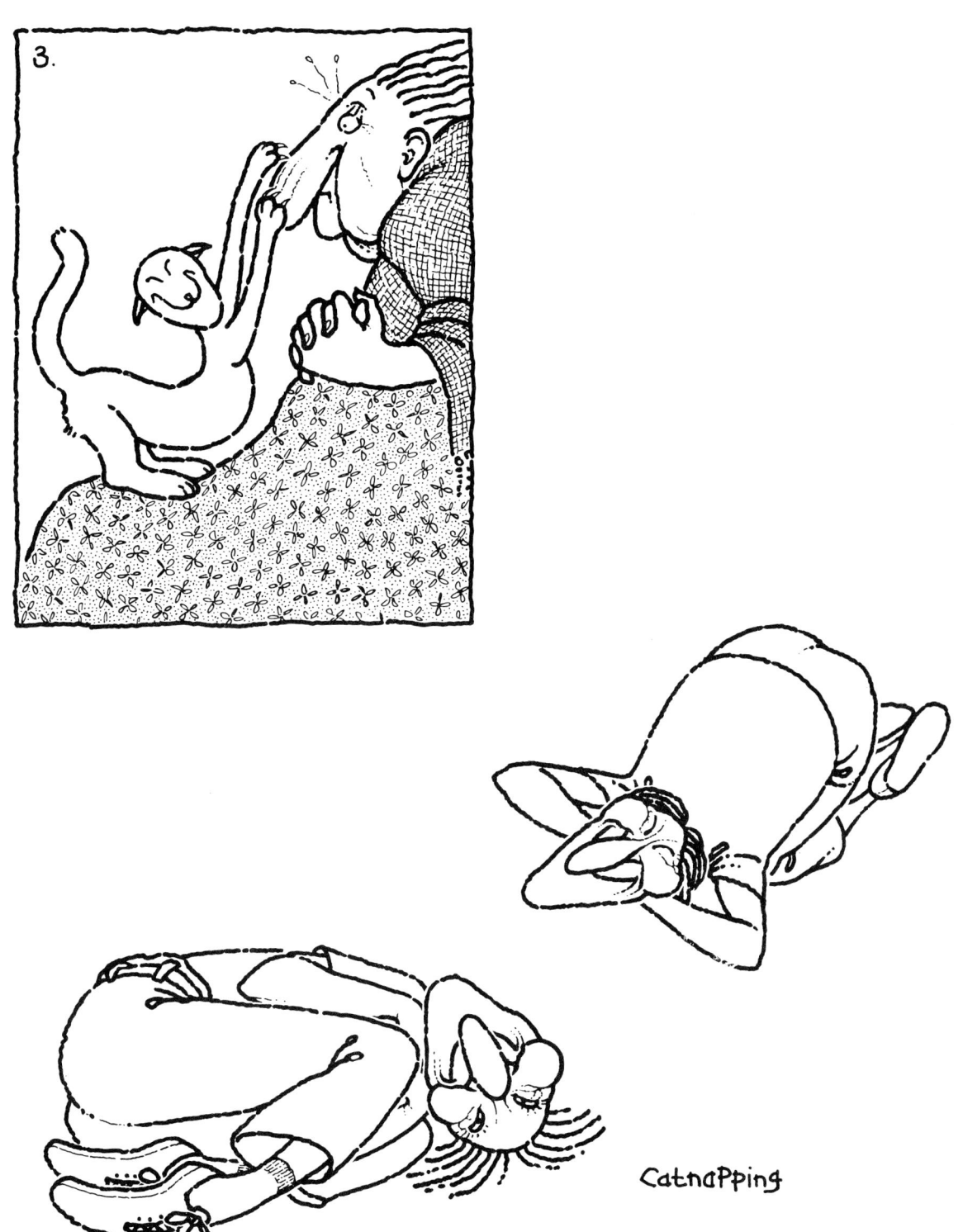

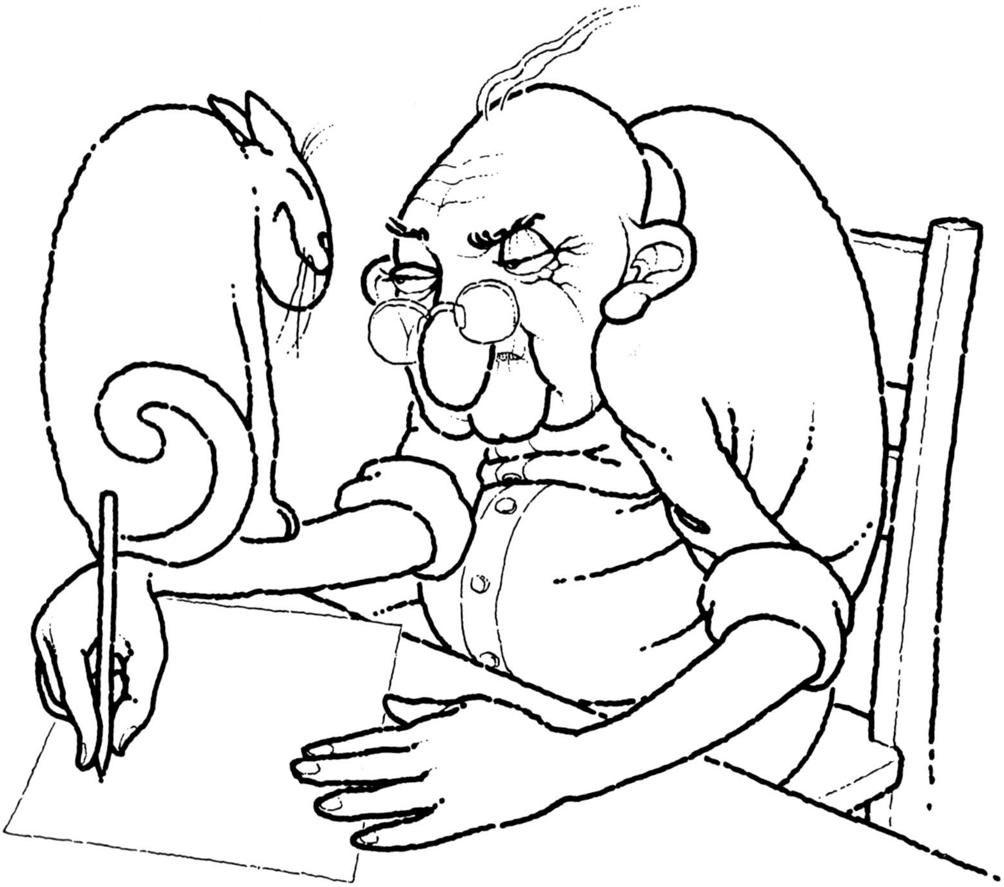

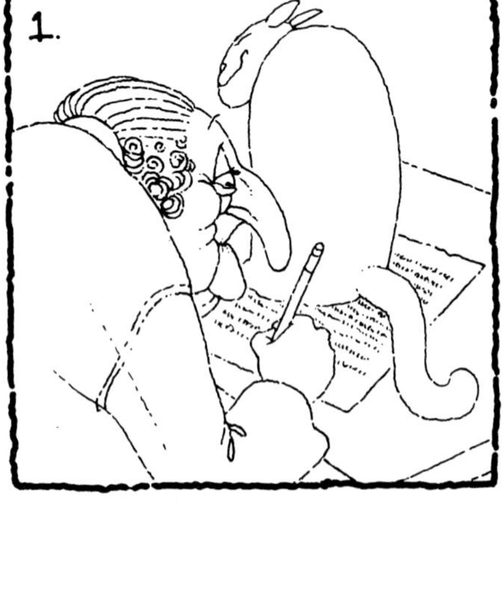
1.

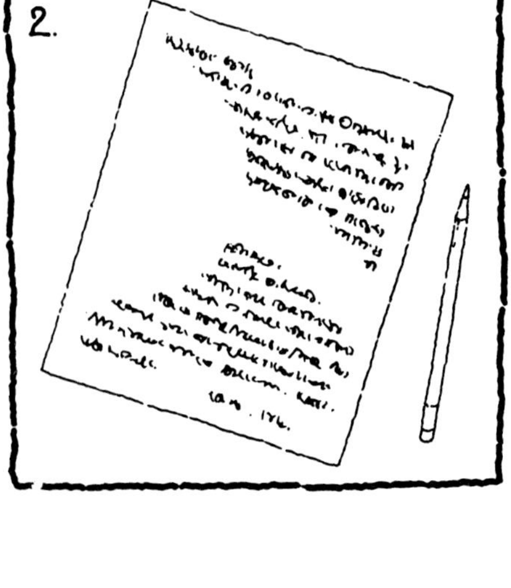
2.

caveman discovering prehistoric cat hair

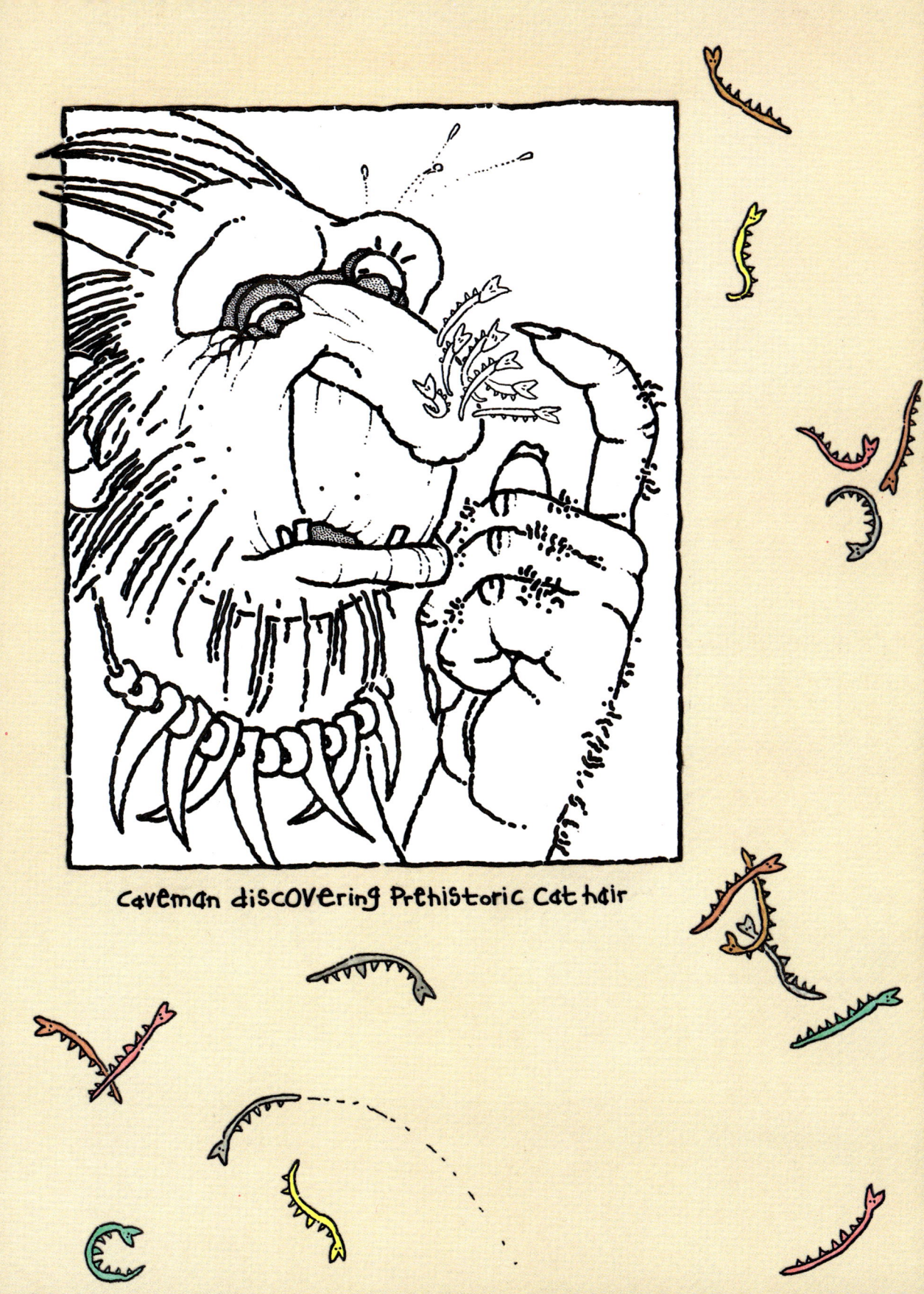

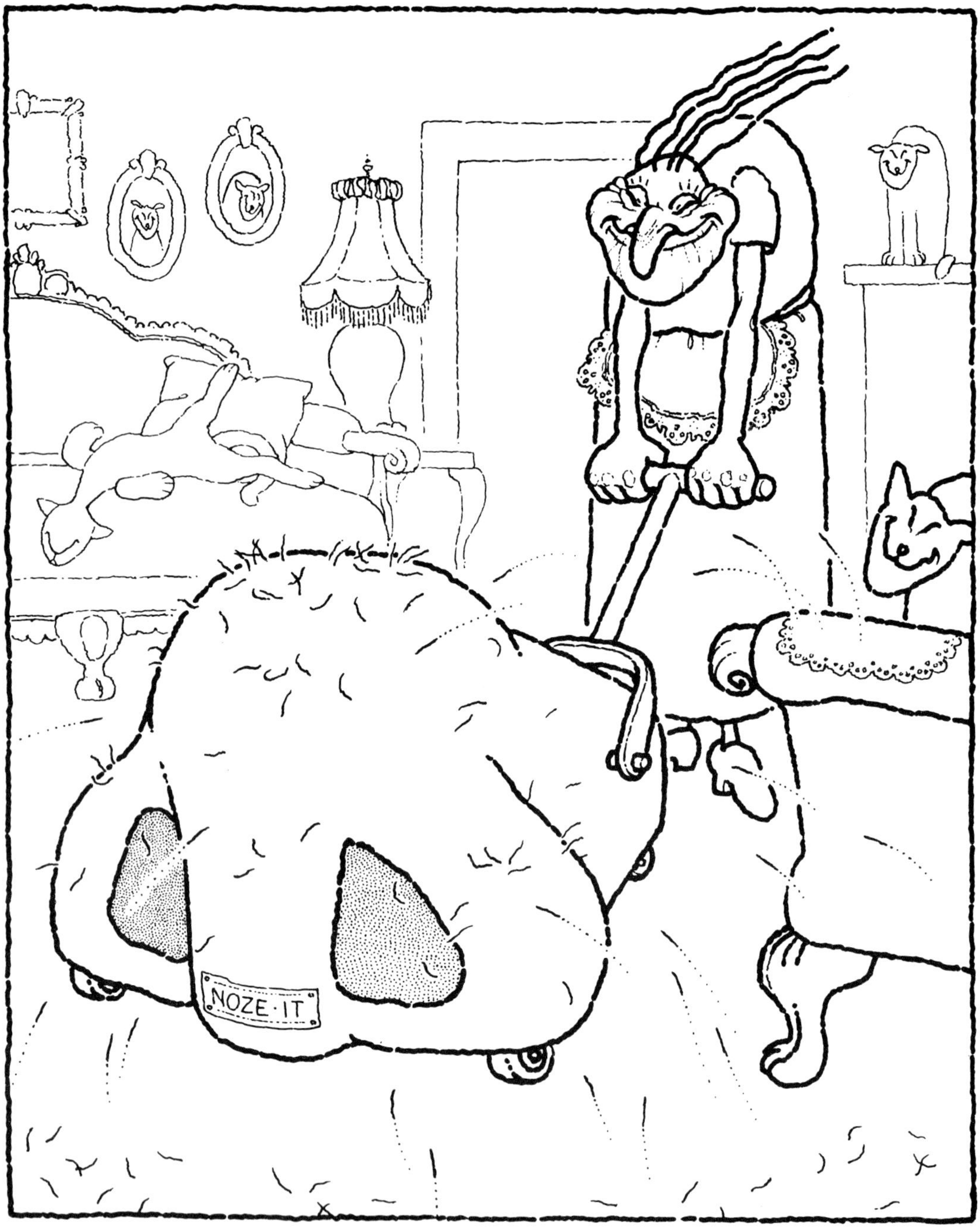
NOZE·IT

cat hairs jumping on the lifelike 'noze·it' cat hair eliminator

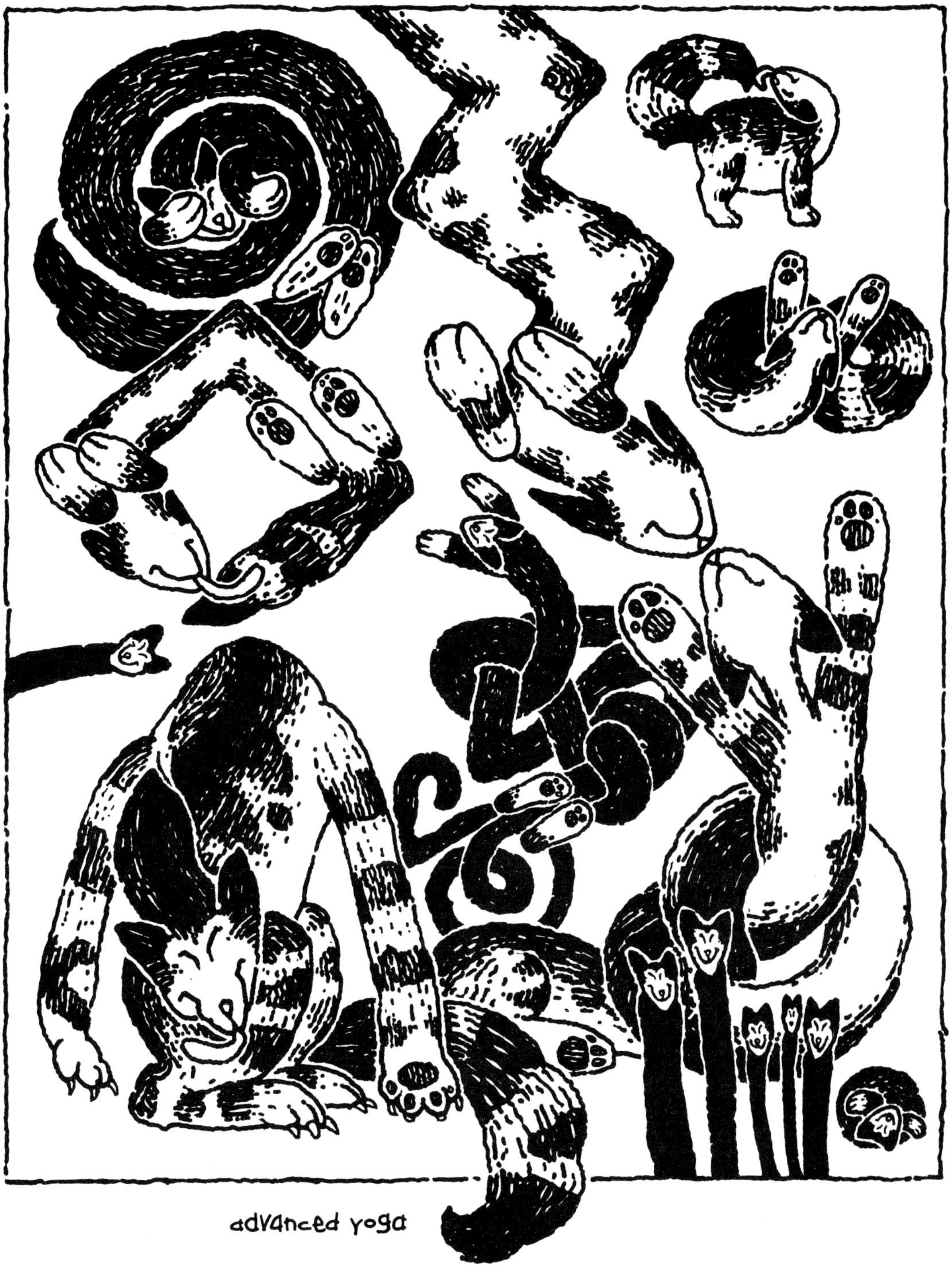

advanced yoga

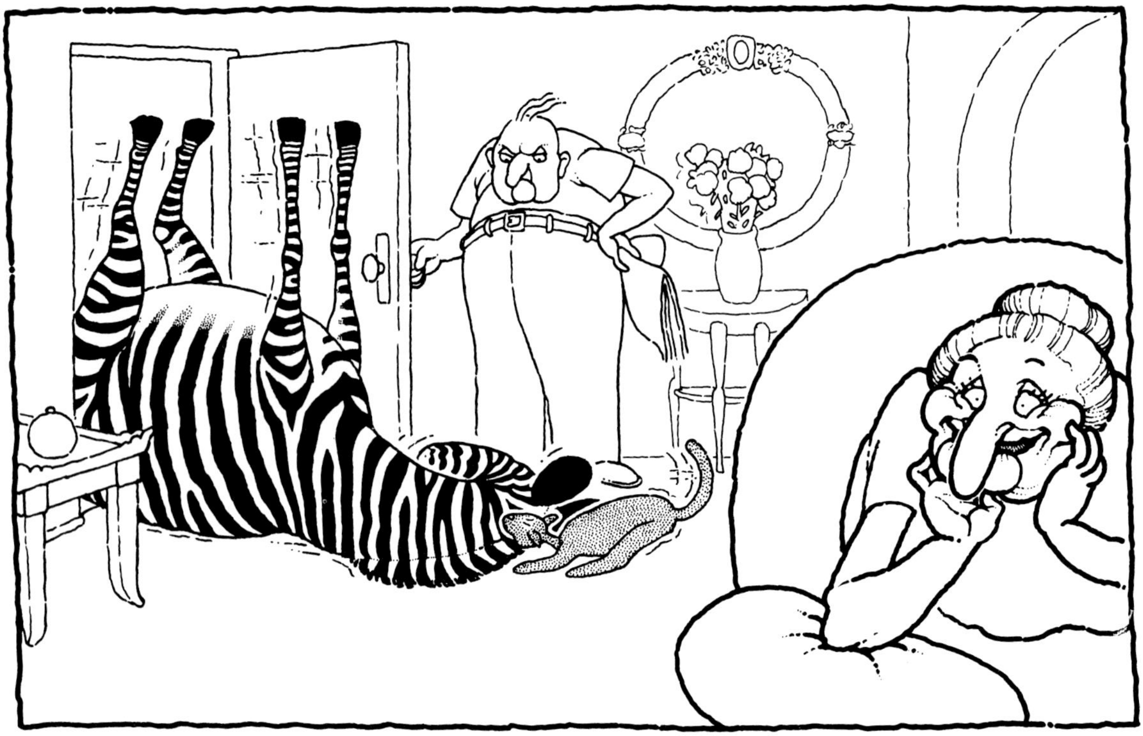

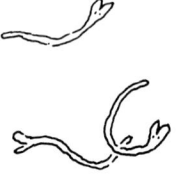

"did that naughty muffin of mine bring us another little present? no kitty kandy for you tonight muffin, you naughty, naughty girl."

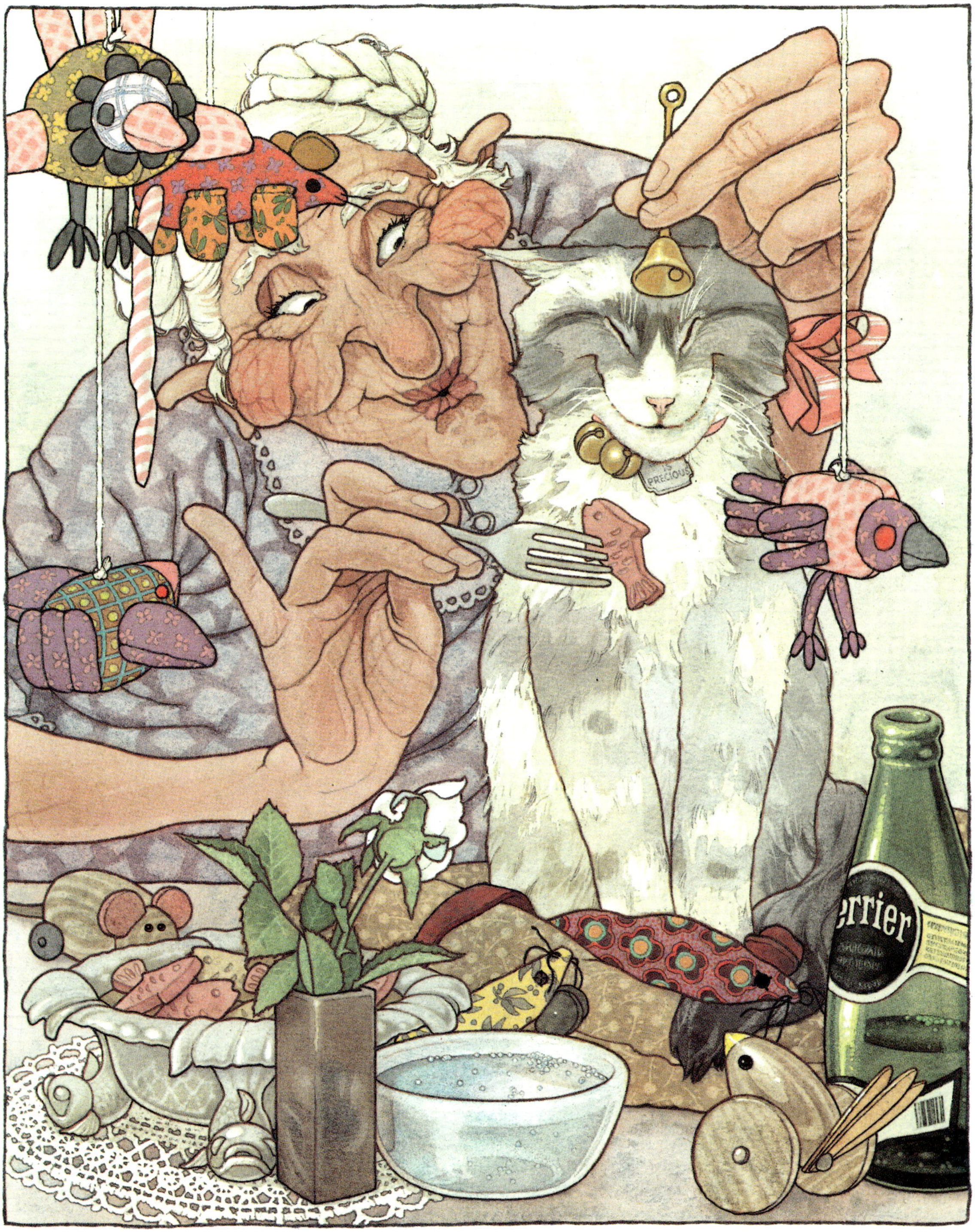
PRECIOUS
errier

fish treats for Precious

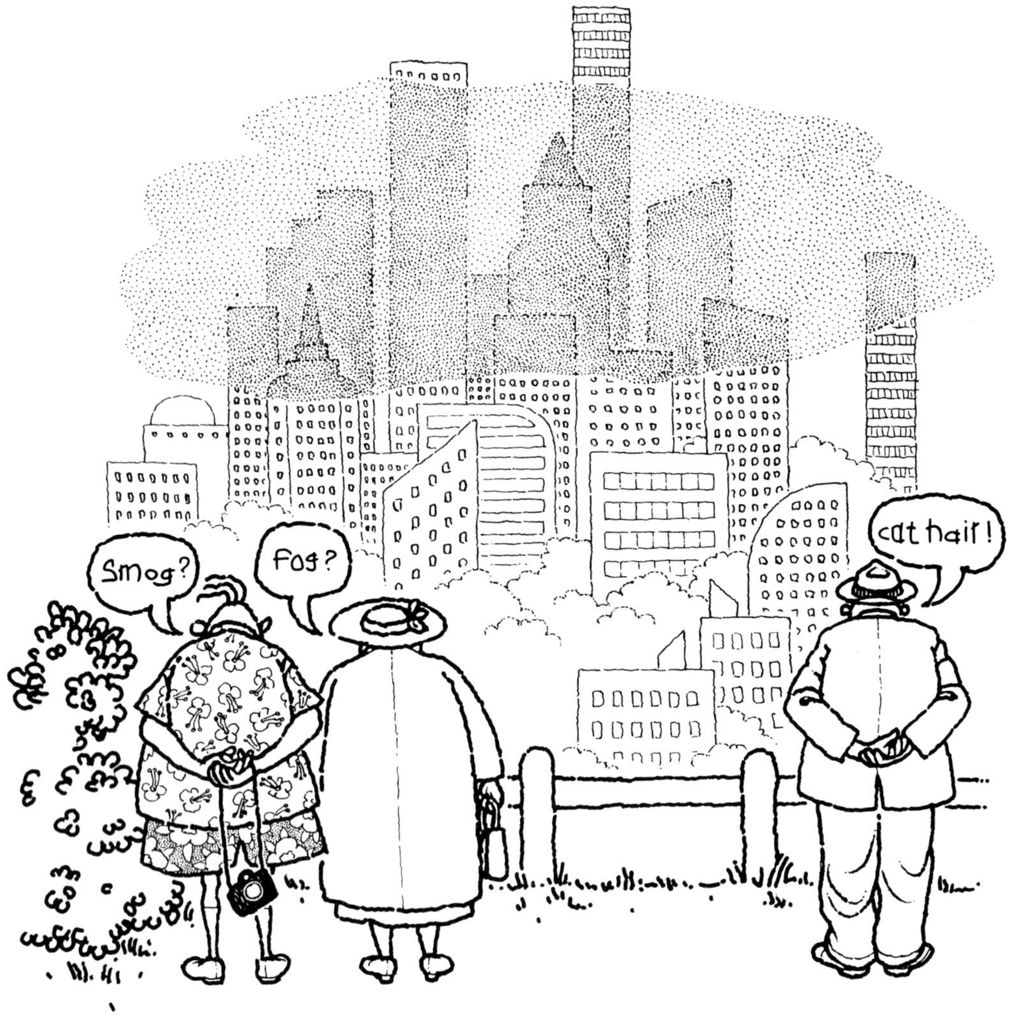
Smog?
Fog?
cat hair!

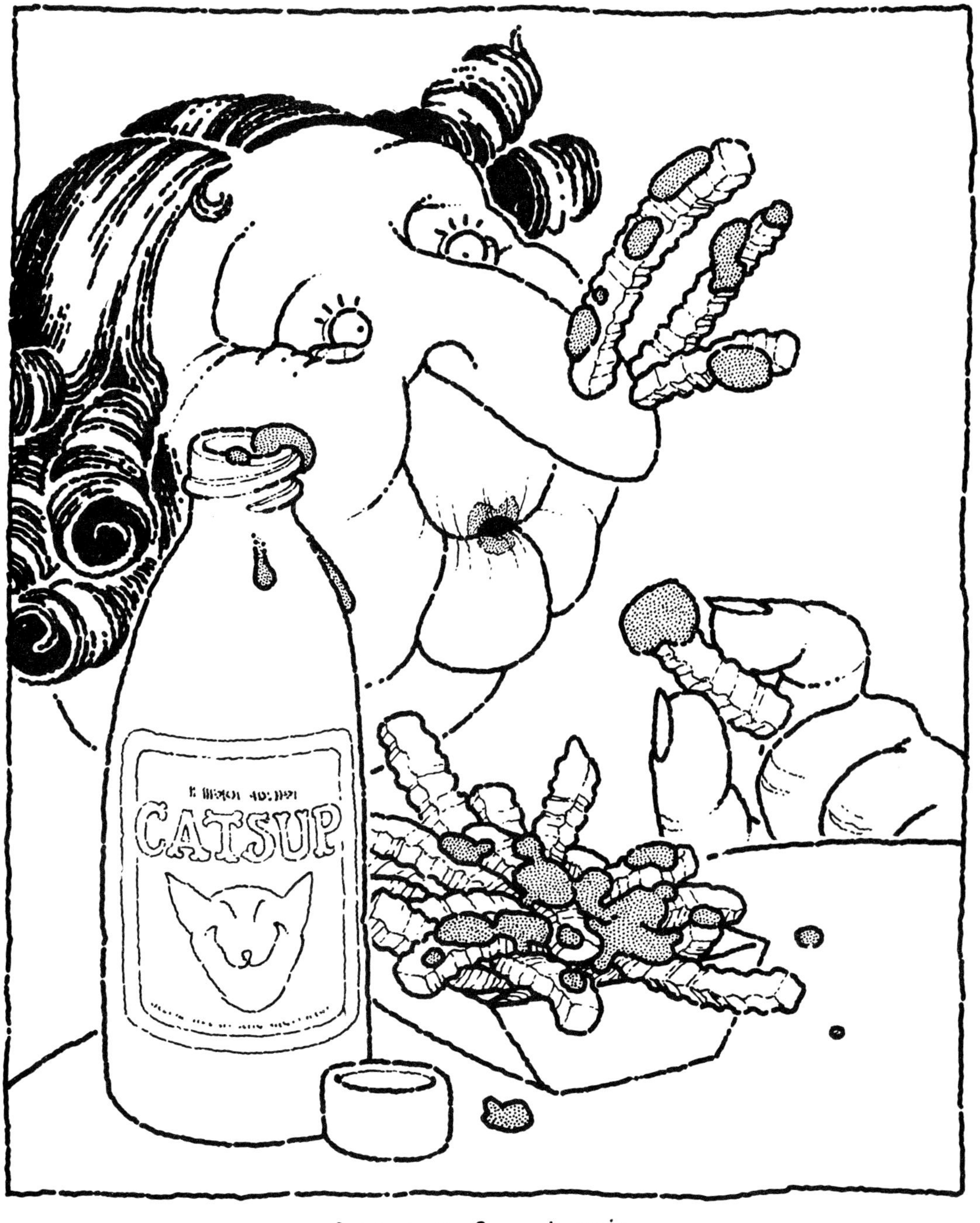
CATSUP

Catsup on french fries

1.

2.

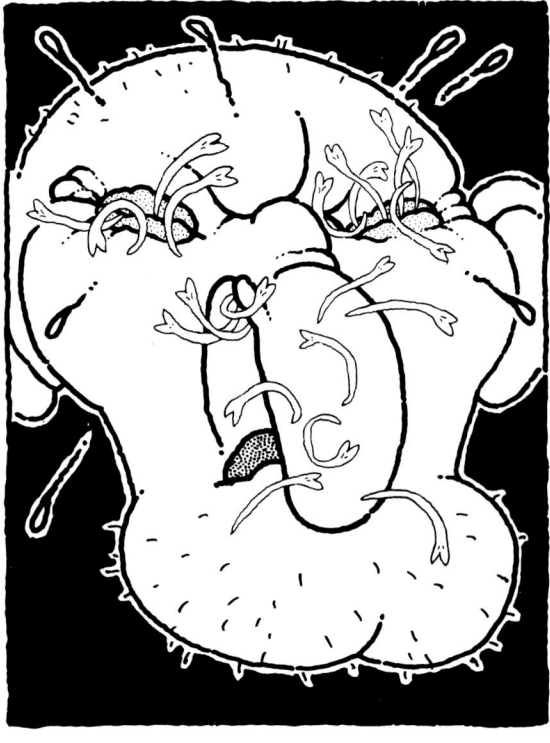

"So wudda ya gunna do about it copper? sic da Puddie cop on me? har, har, har."

"does your cat shed? do you have cat hair build up? then you need Puddie Pleez Pitchfork. new from Puddie Pleez Pet Products."

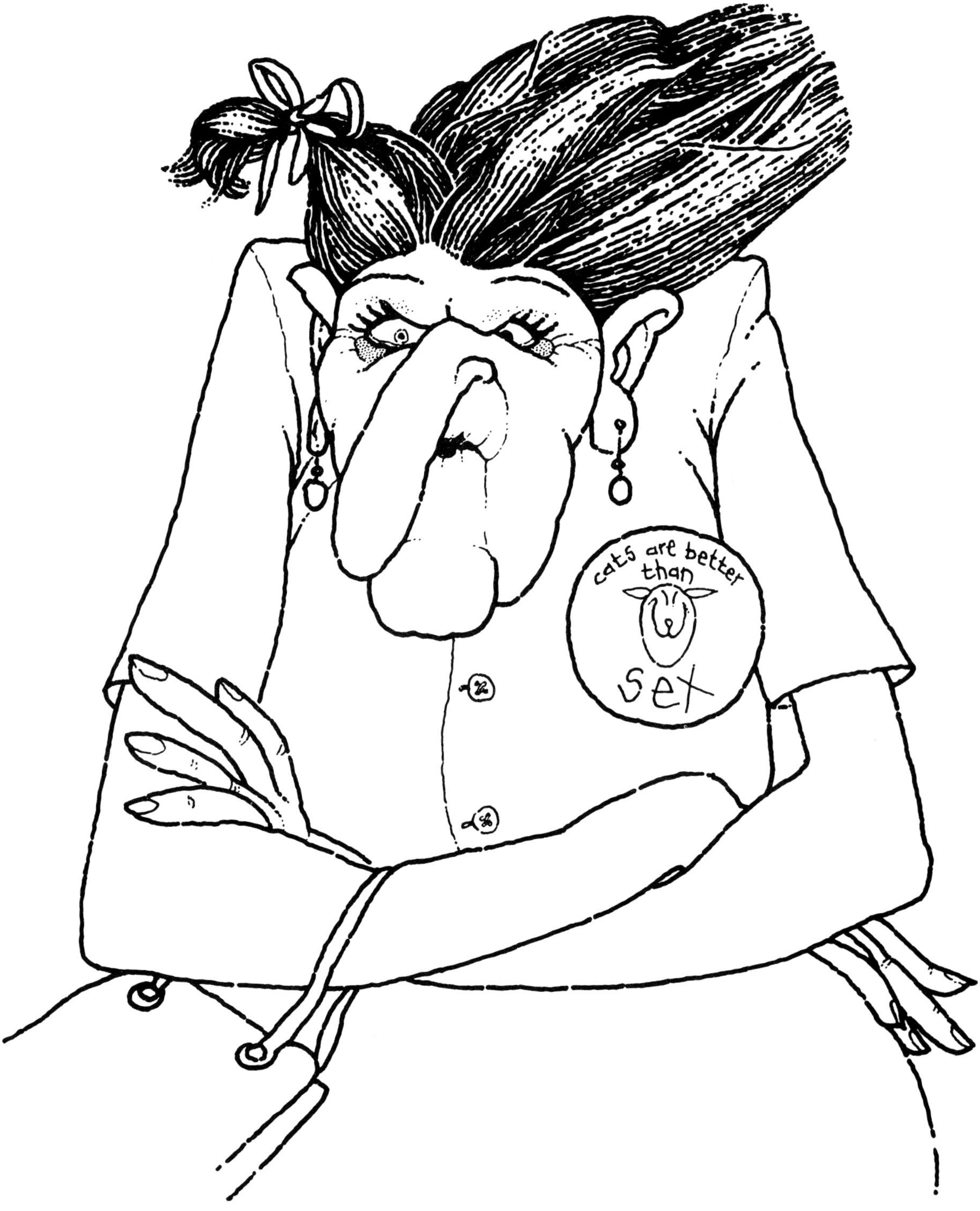
cats are better than
sex

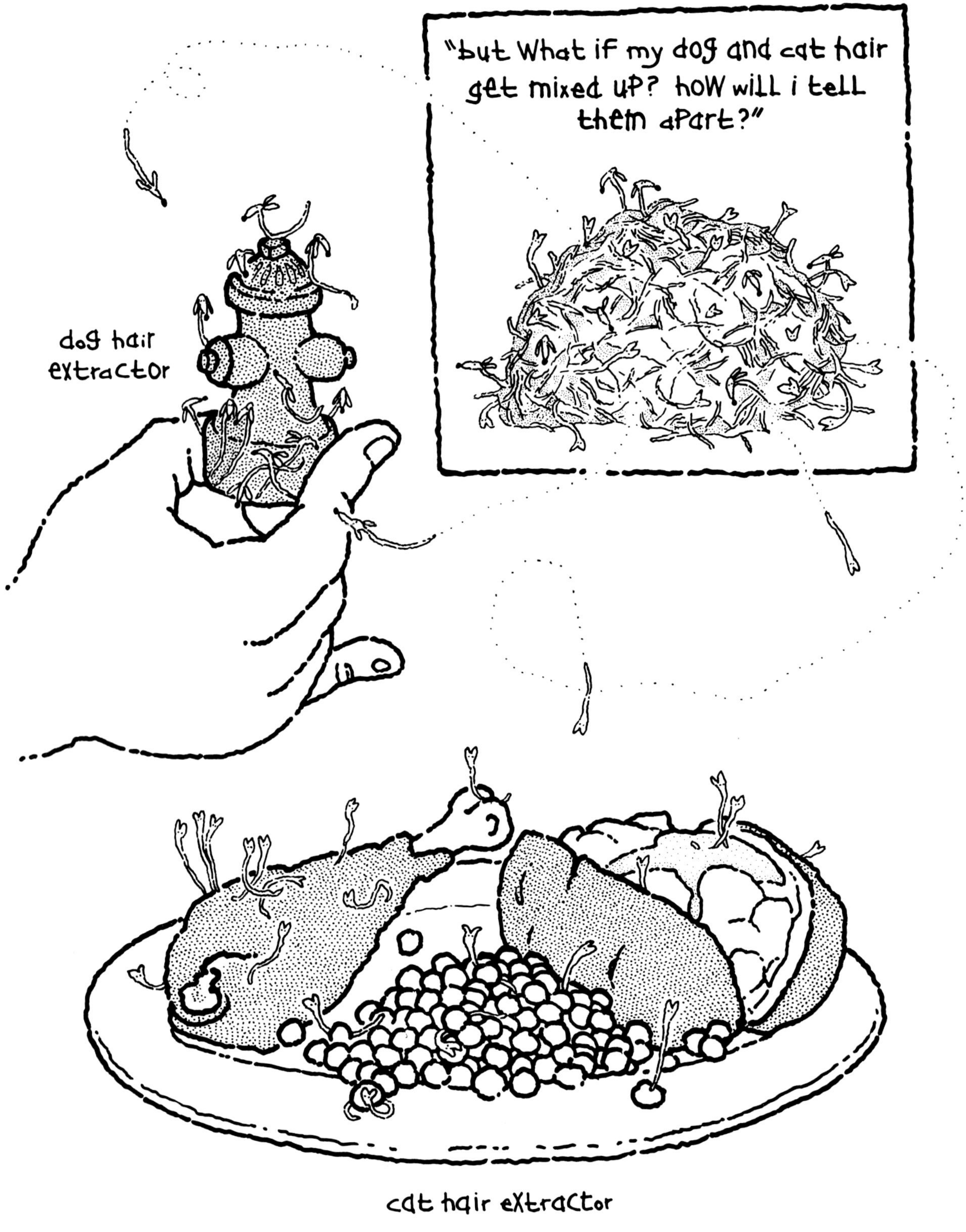
"but What if my dog and cat hair get mixed up? how will i tell them apart?"
dog hair extractor
cat hair extractor

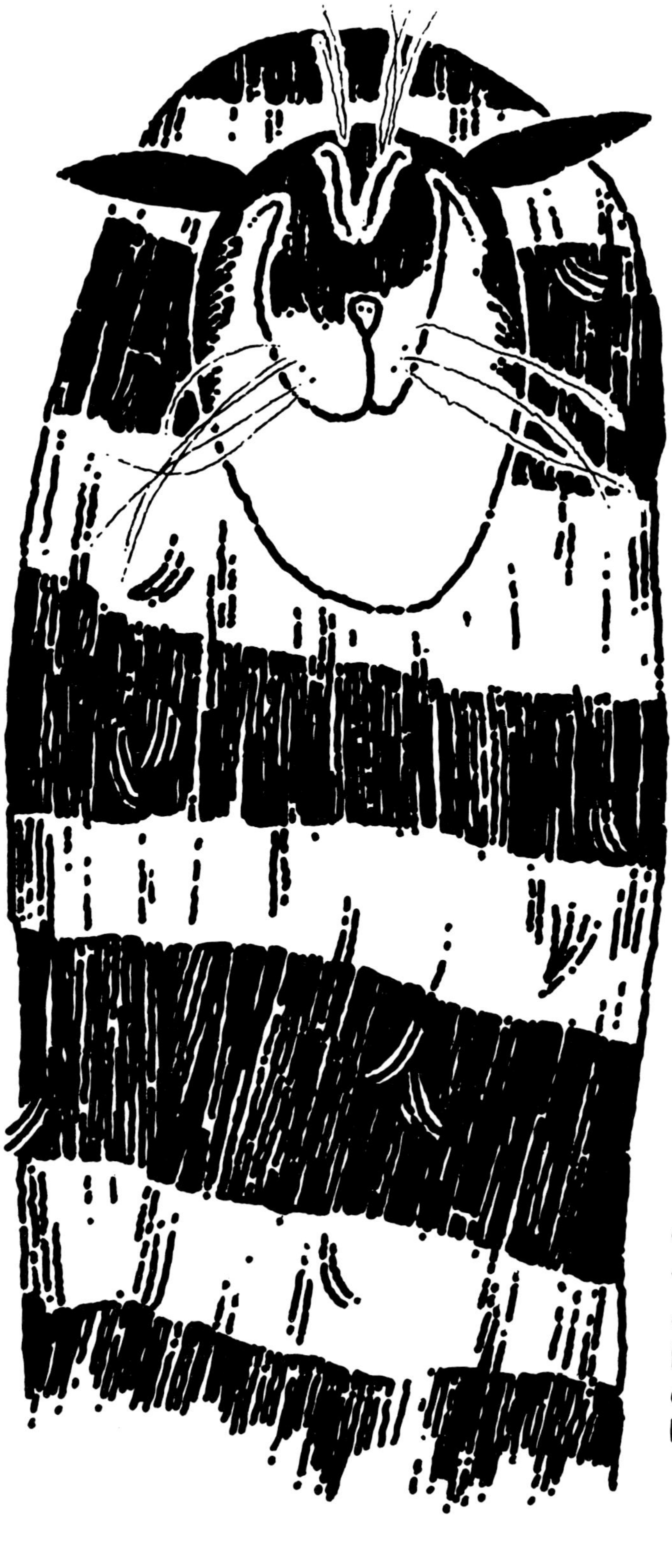

Cat
thinking
an extremely
important thought
about
hoover dam

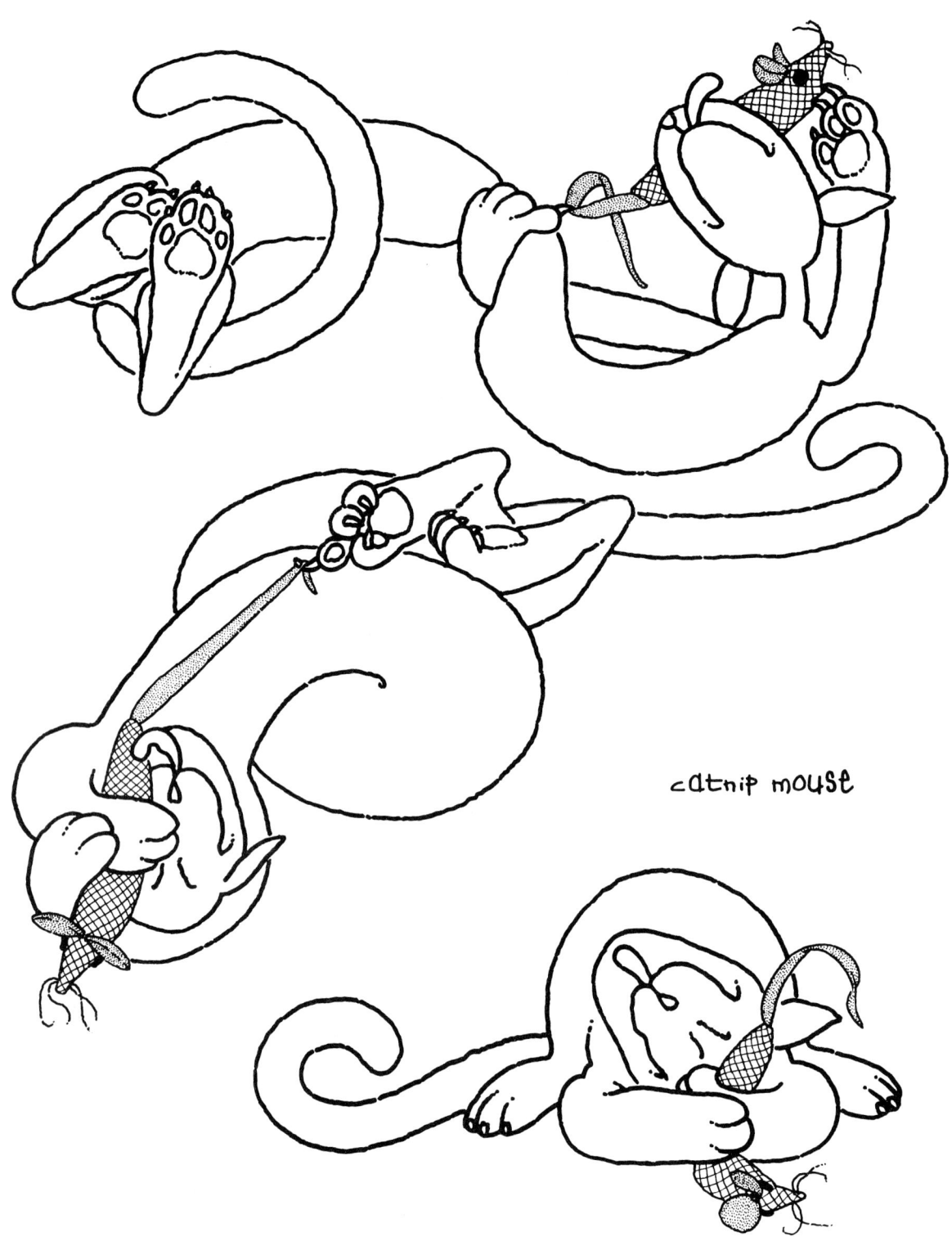

catnip mouse

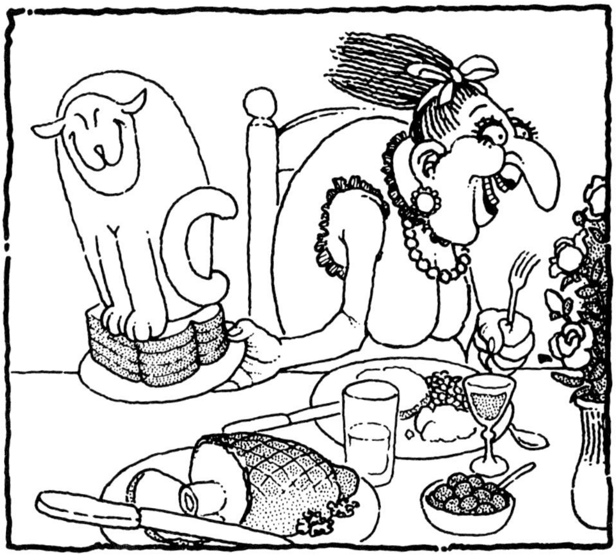

"would anyone care for another slice of bread?"

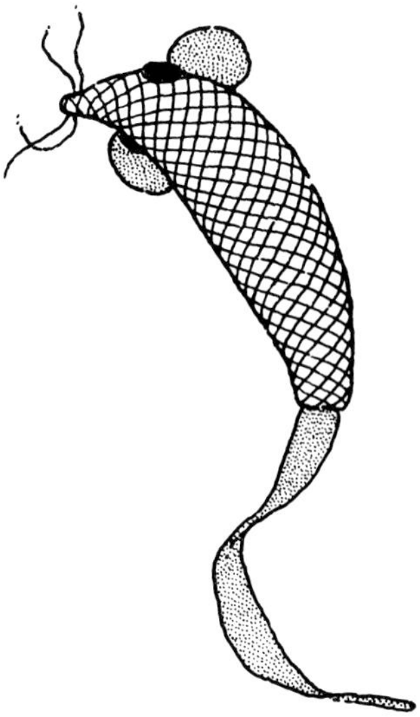

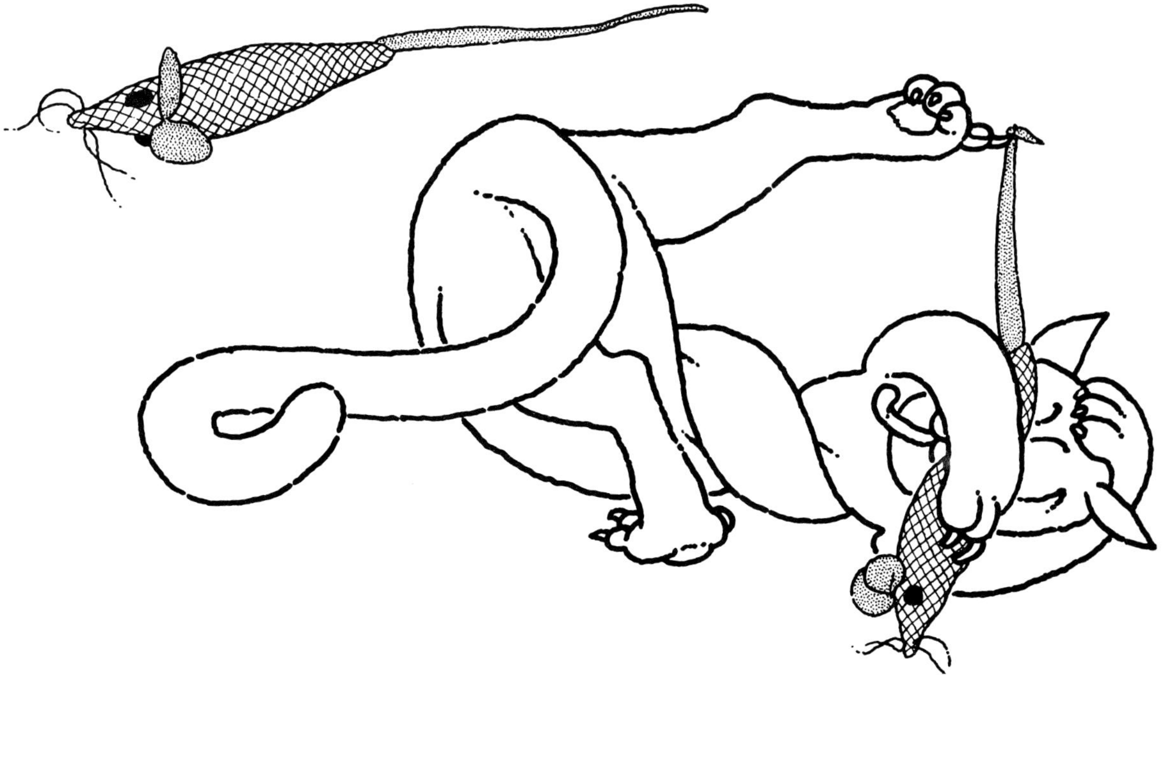

how to fold a cat

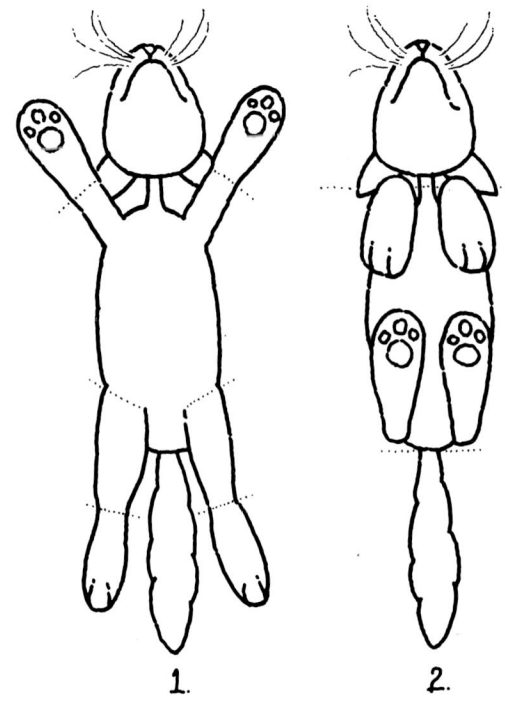

1.   2.

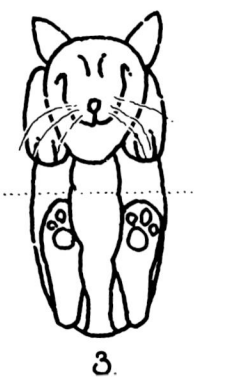

3.

4.

- compact for traveling.
- stack your extra cats for easy carrying or storage.
- slip one into your purse or briefcase.
- fits into standard 9 x 12" envelope for easy mailing.
- simply unfold and they're ready to use.

- or store your extra cats on the bookshelf when not in use.

caution: do not try this on your dog. dogs do not fold well.

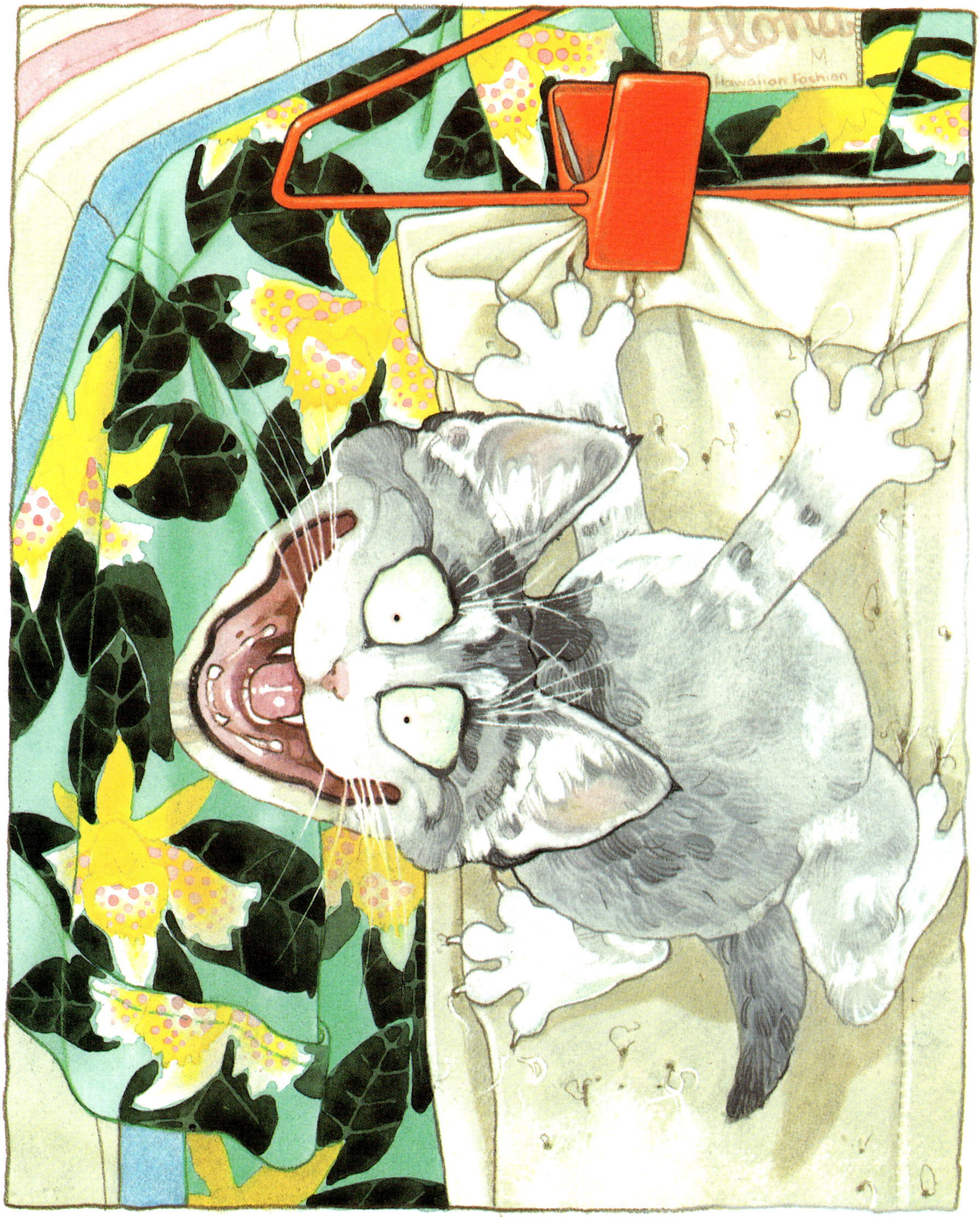
Aloha
M
Hawaiian Fashion

Little Lulu explores the closet

Cat,
having
become the medium
through which the
dead Albert Einstein
speaks,
prepares to
field questions
should
there be any further
inquiries about
relativity

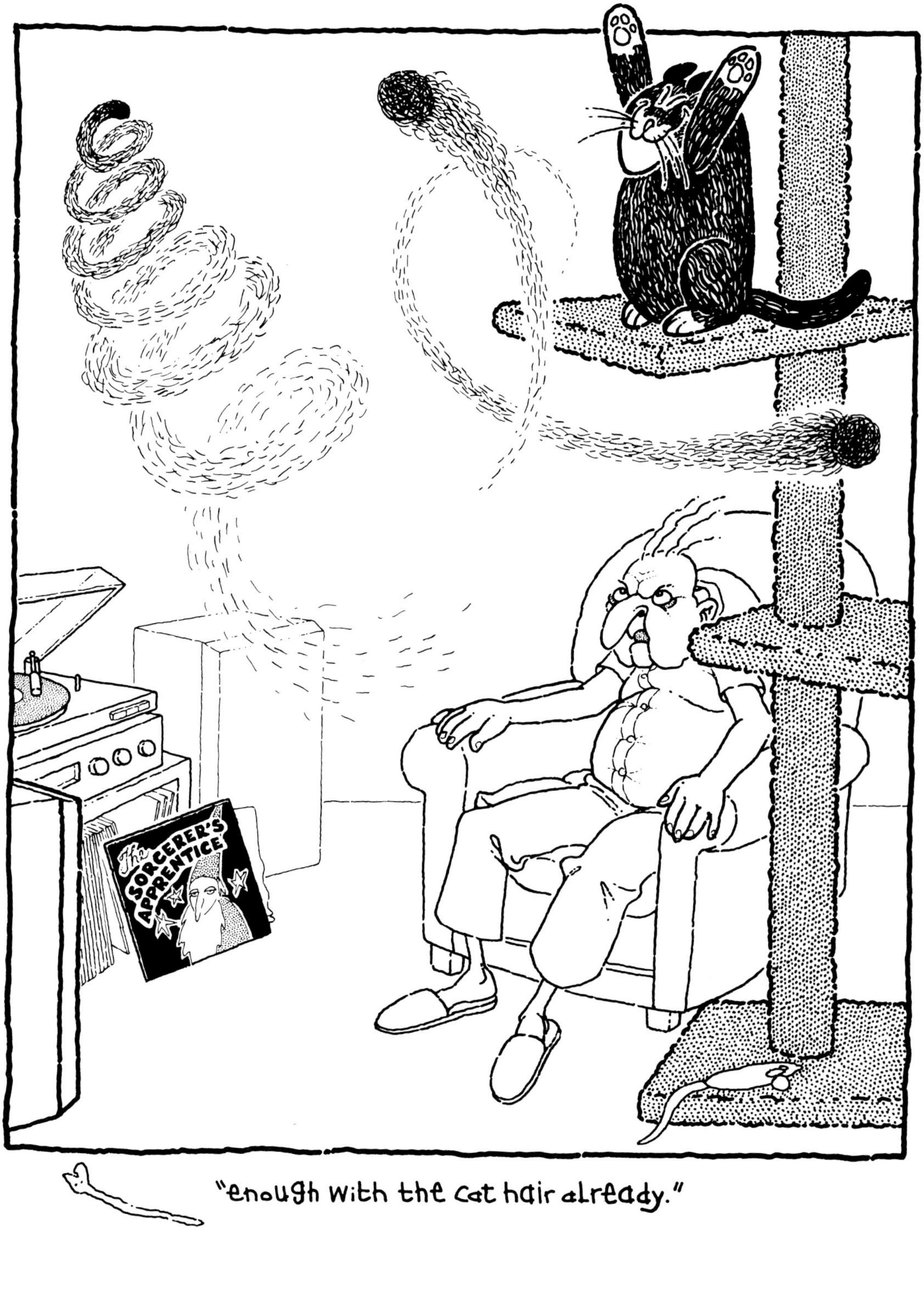
The SORCERER'S APPRENTICE
"enough with the cat hair already."

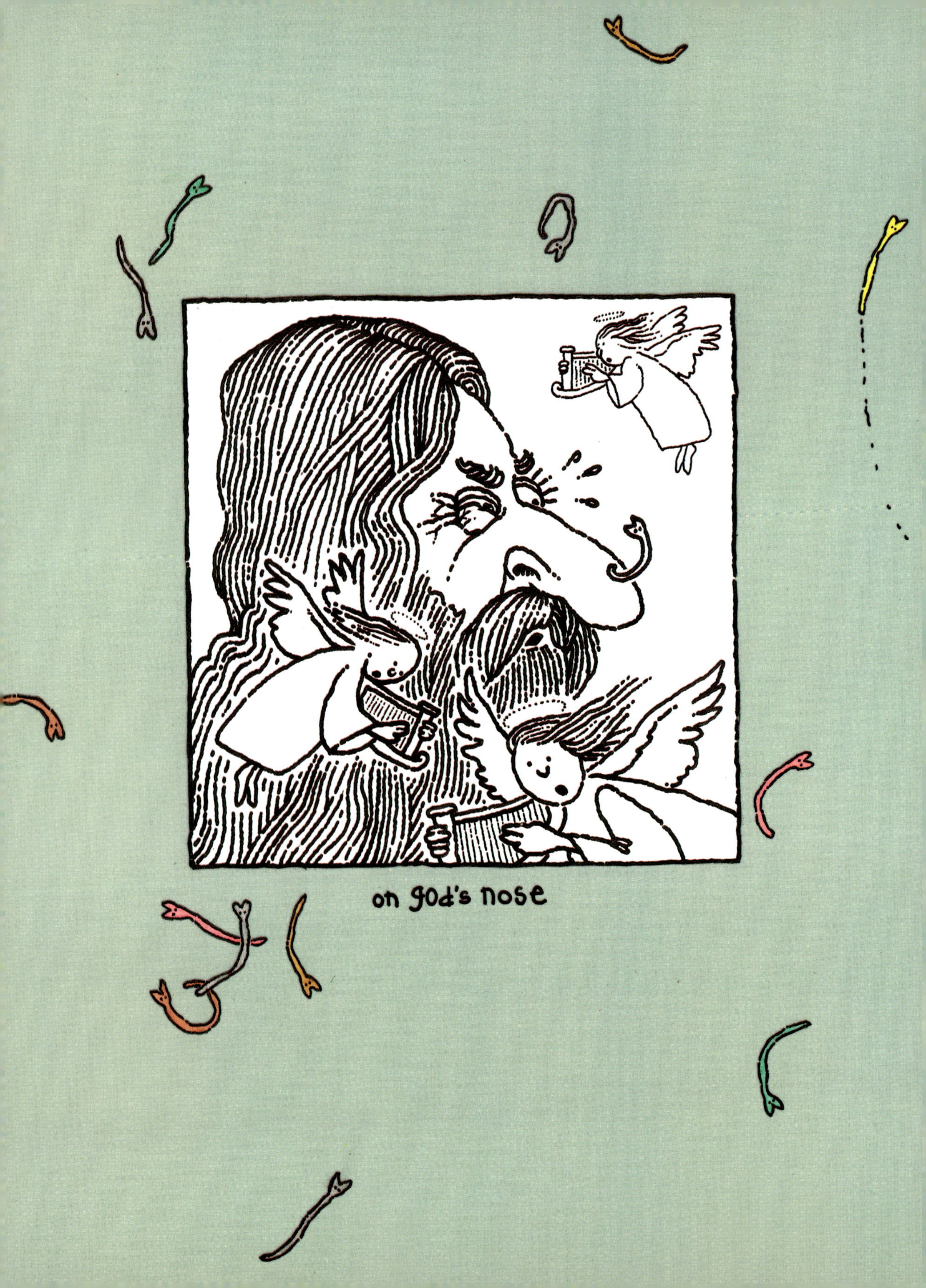

on god's nose

"Yes, it's true that your wonderful NOZE·IT Scarecrow and NOZE·IT Dog Spot have made me the most popular man in town. And, of course, it's also true that NOZE·IT has made my nose cat hair and bird-free. But sometimes I don't want to be the center of attention. Can you help me?"

Derf Nalpak, Illinois

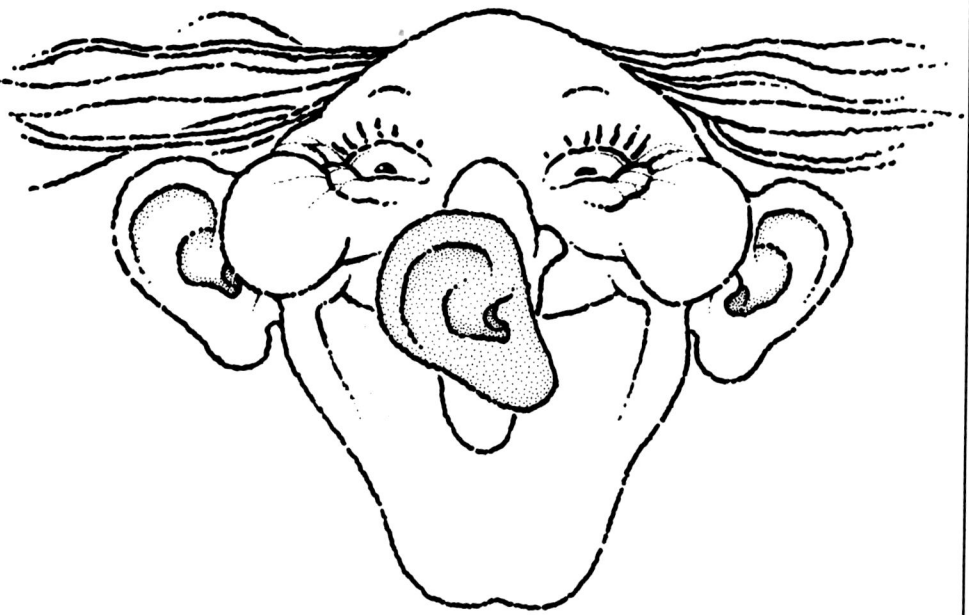

You've asked for it and now here it is! Cat hairs as well as people will stay away from you in droves when you wear our new NOZE·ITeer. It's true! It's been proven in laboratory tests. Cat hairs are fooled into thinking that you have no nose at all! – that you actually have three ears!!! You heard right. Be a Three NOZE·ITeer. Sets of three earrings are also available for the ladies. Write for catalog.

It really works! We NOZE·IT works.

NOZE·IT · Attn: NOZE·ITeer Dept. · Cat Hair Rd. · Nose, CA 86222

the transformation of
ferdy and curtis

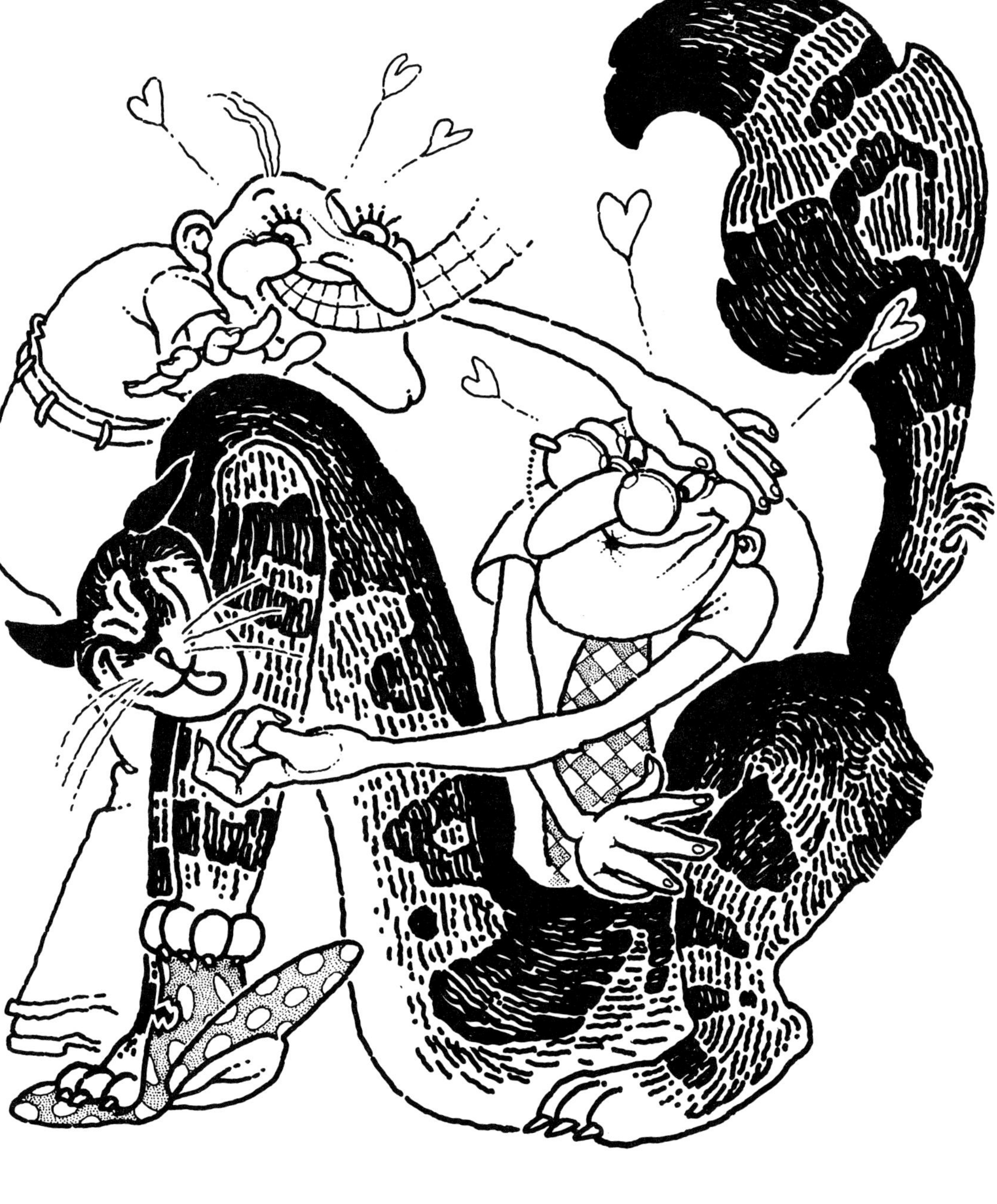

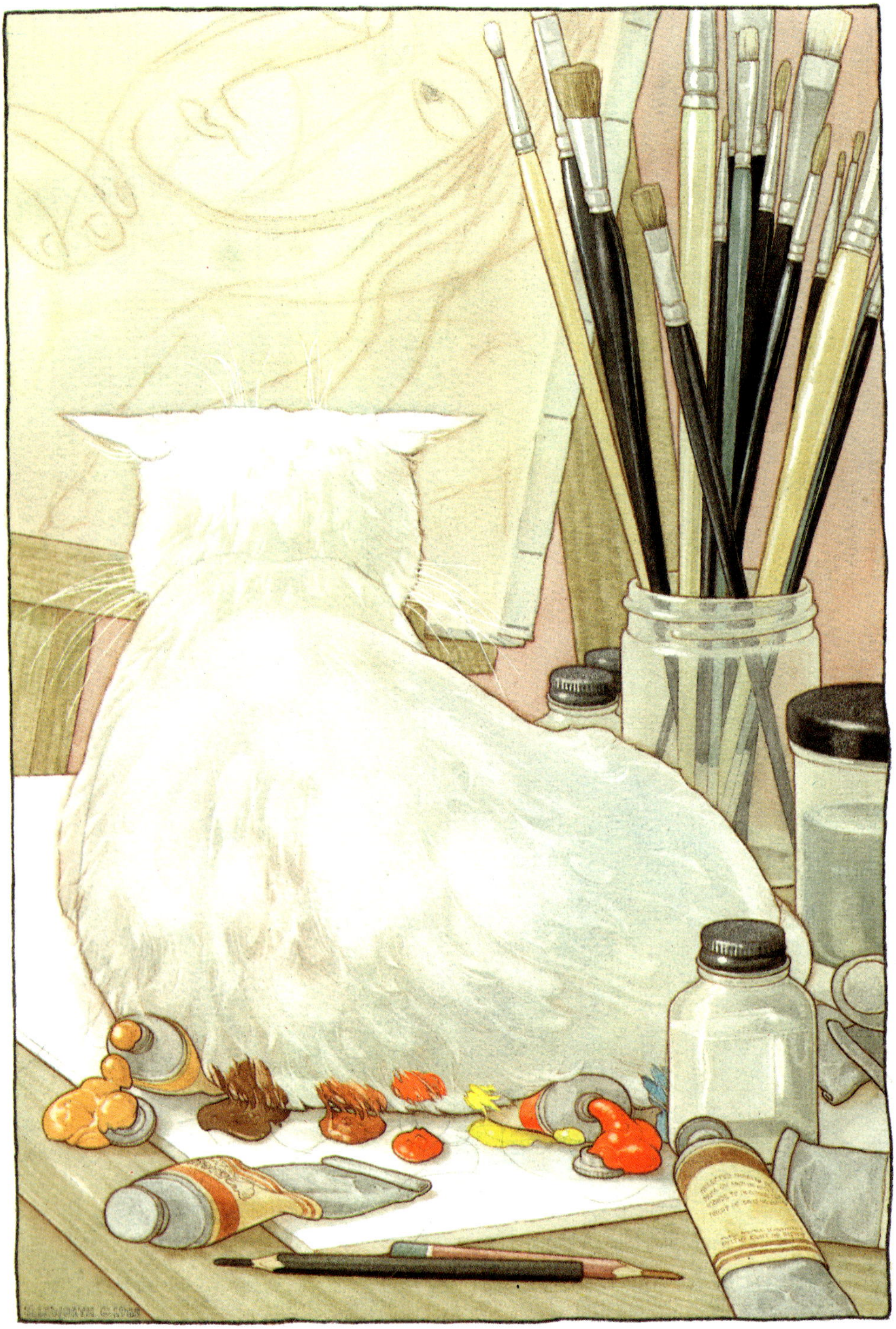

iggy soaks up culture

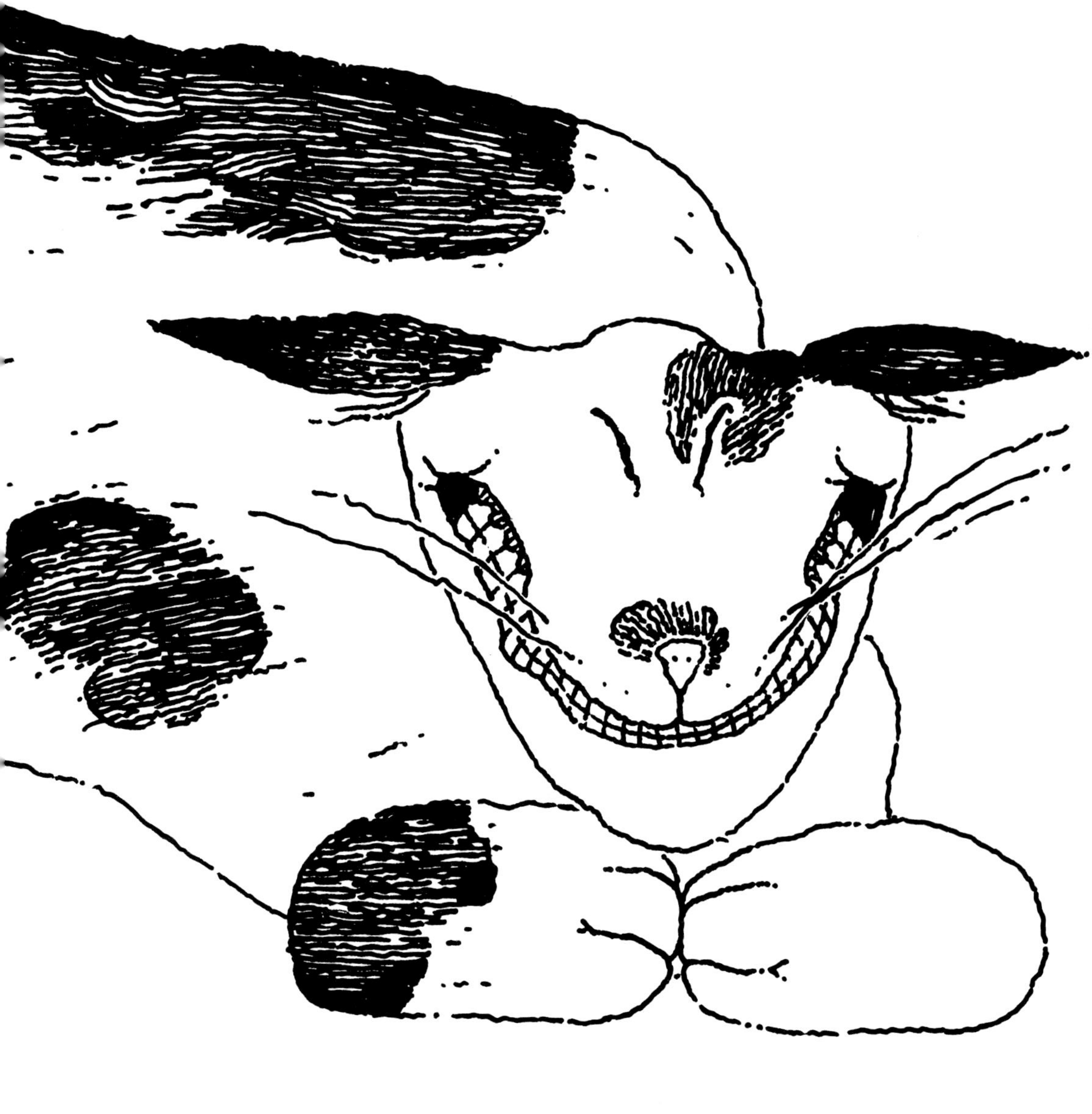

cat caught smiling to itself

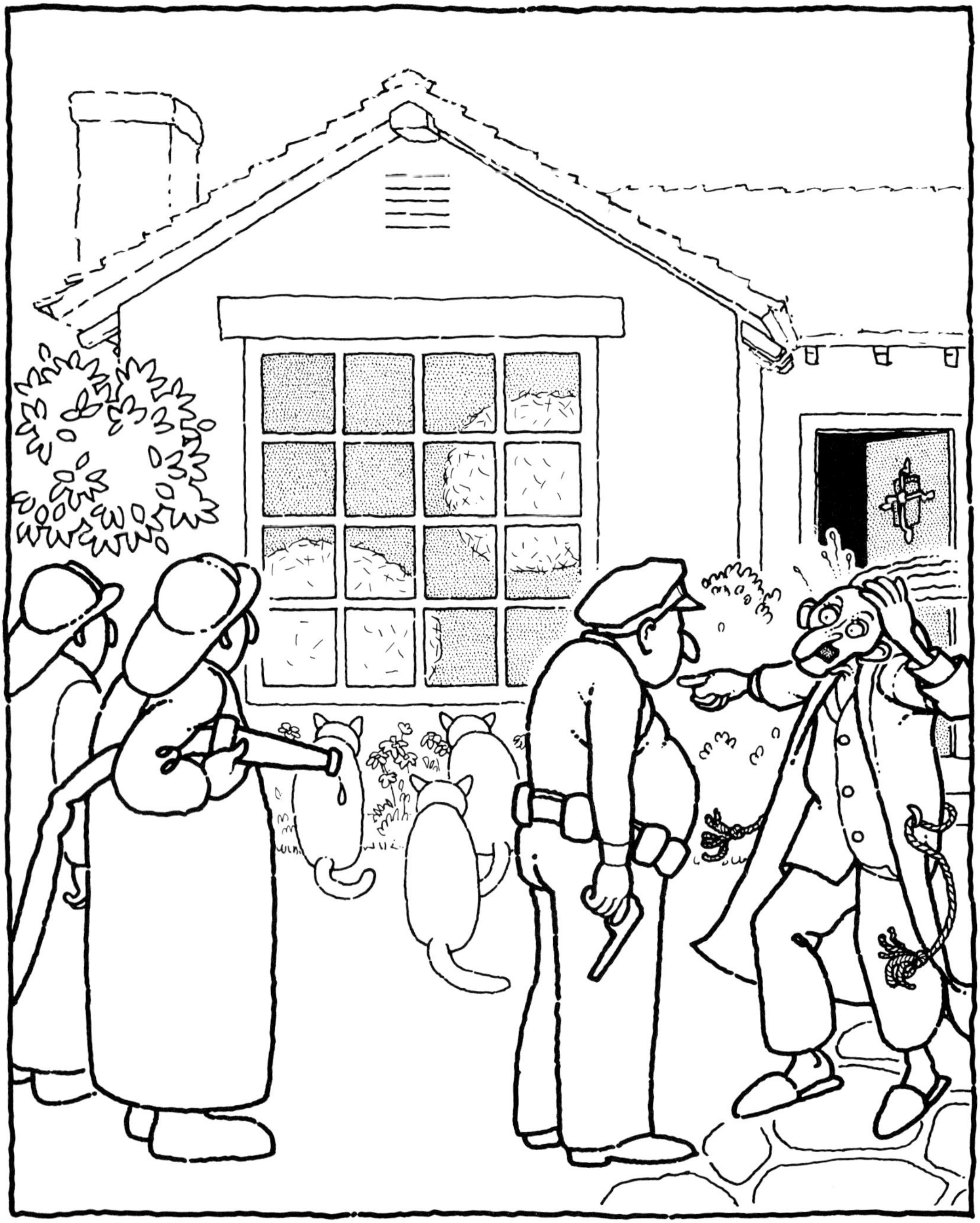

"fur balls!!!"

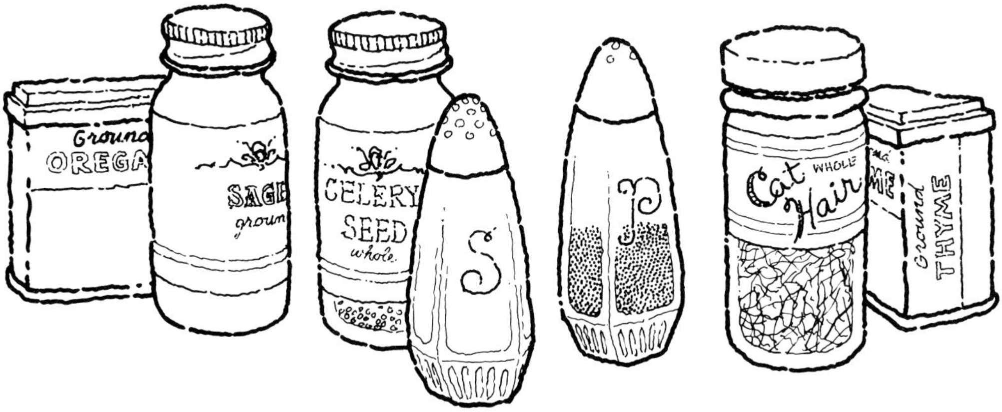
Ground
OREGA
SAGE
groun
CELERY
SEED
whole
S
P
Cat WHOLE
Hair
ME
Ground
THYME

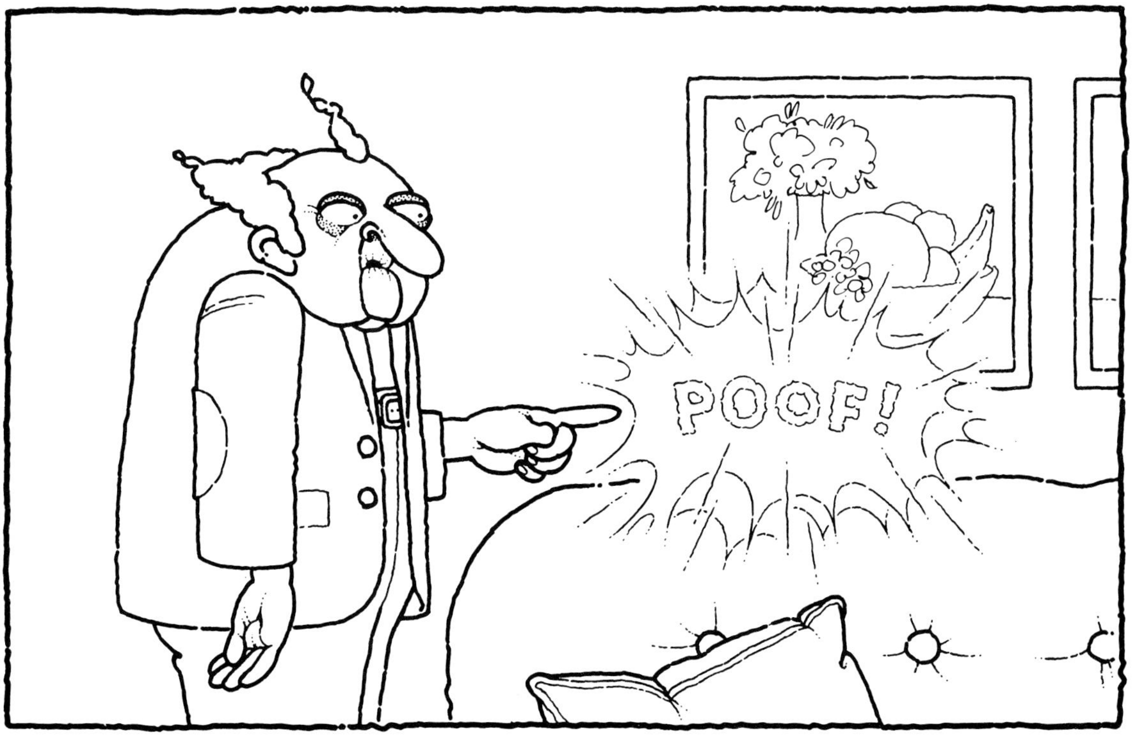
POOF!

never touch a sleeping cat

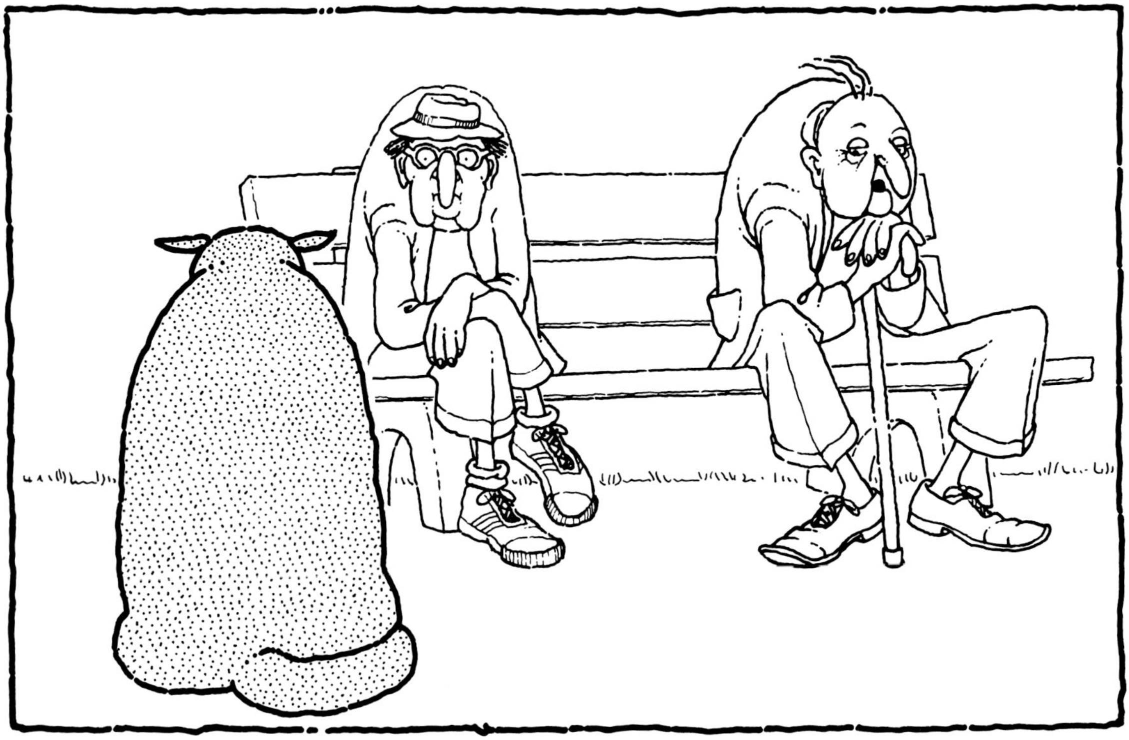

"cats are so real looking"

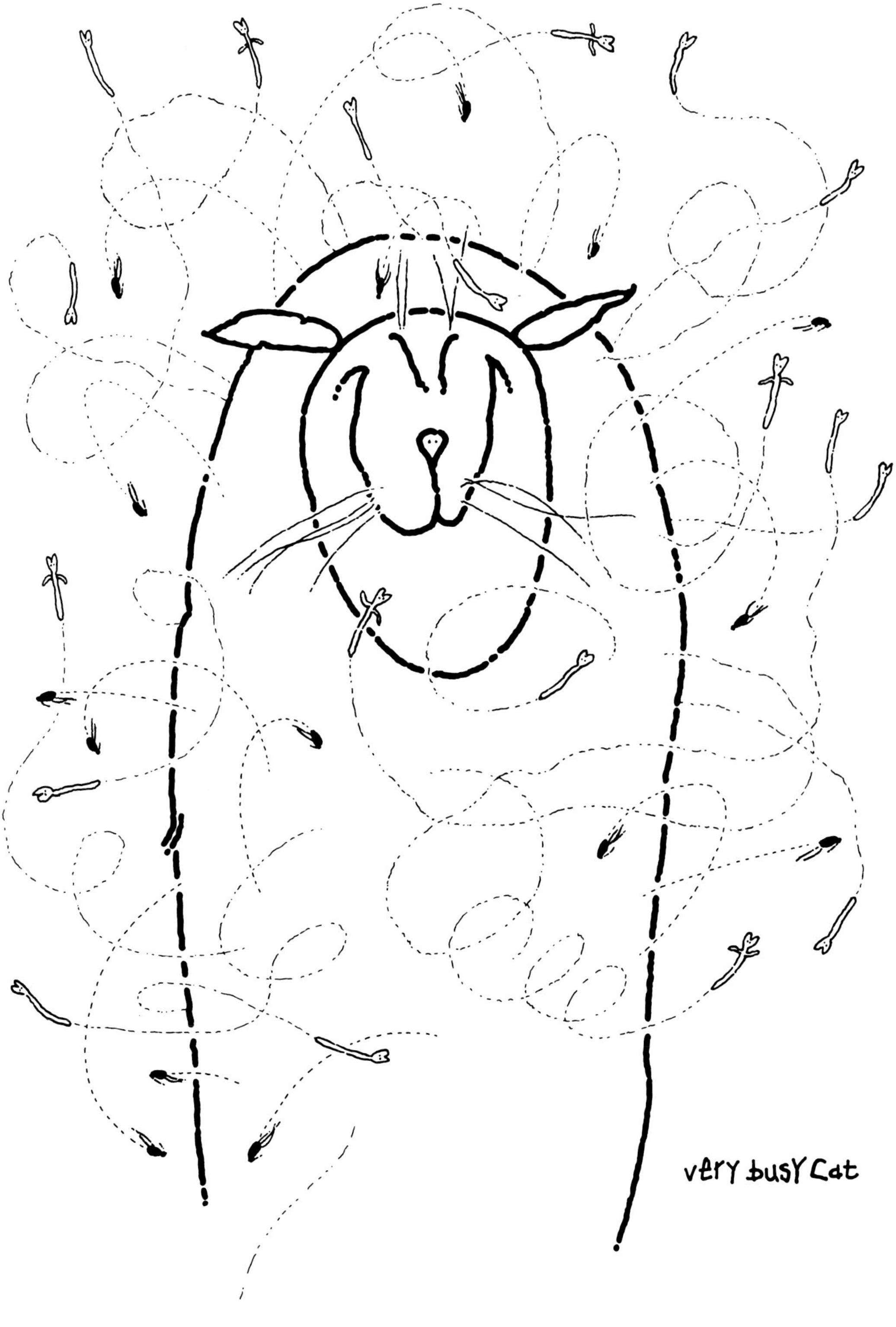

very busy cat

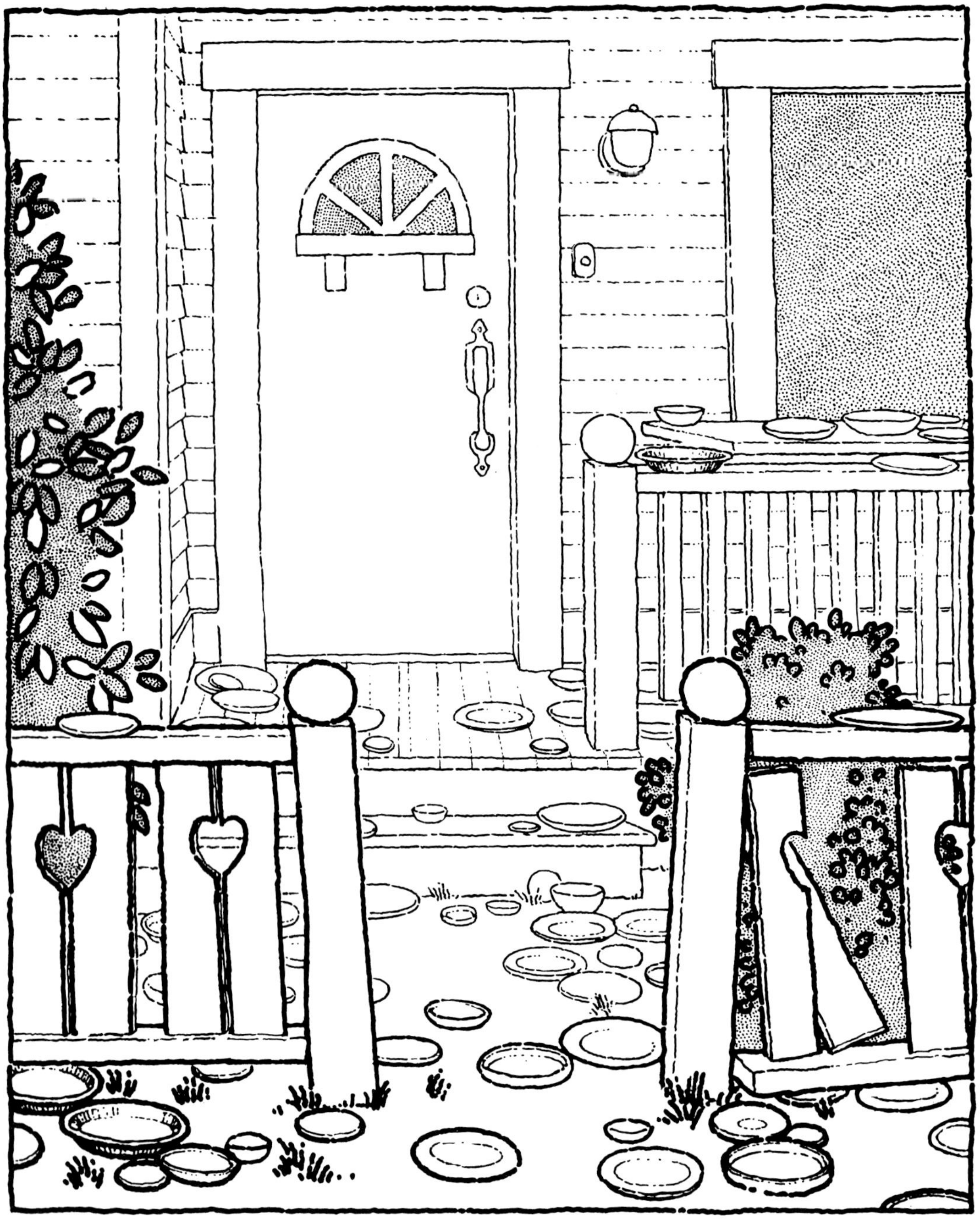

Cat Lady lives here

the Professor attempts to perfect a hairless mechanical cat

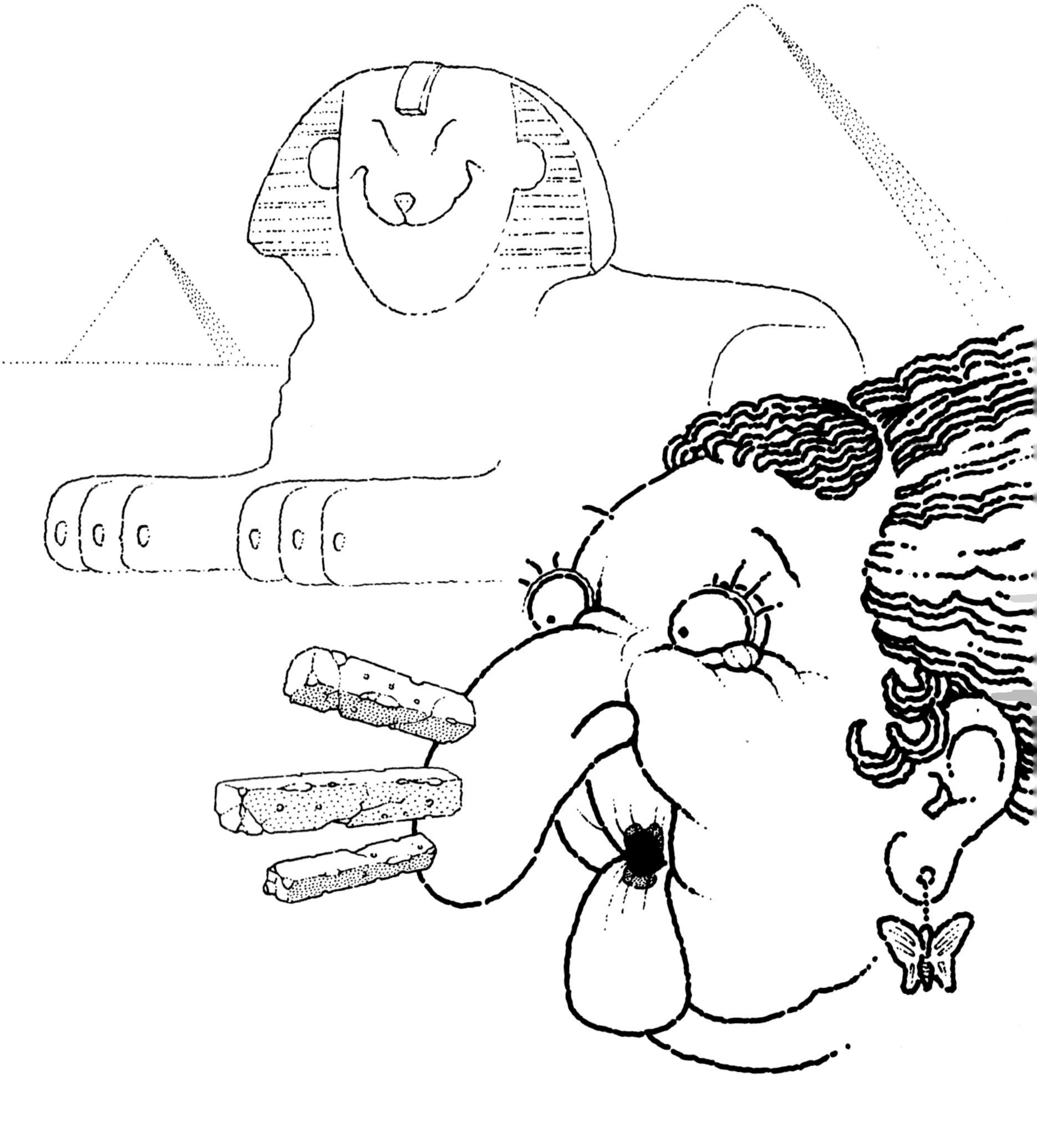

Louise is attacked by Sphinx hairs

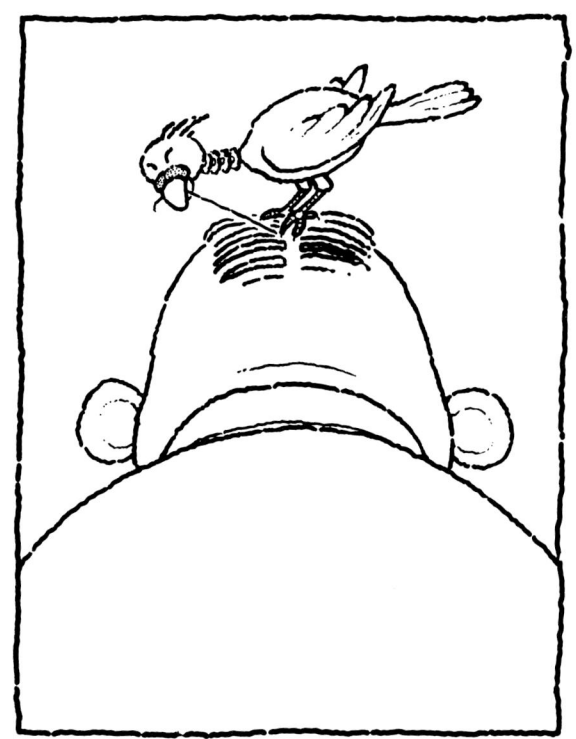

mr. farkle trades in his cat for a Parakeet

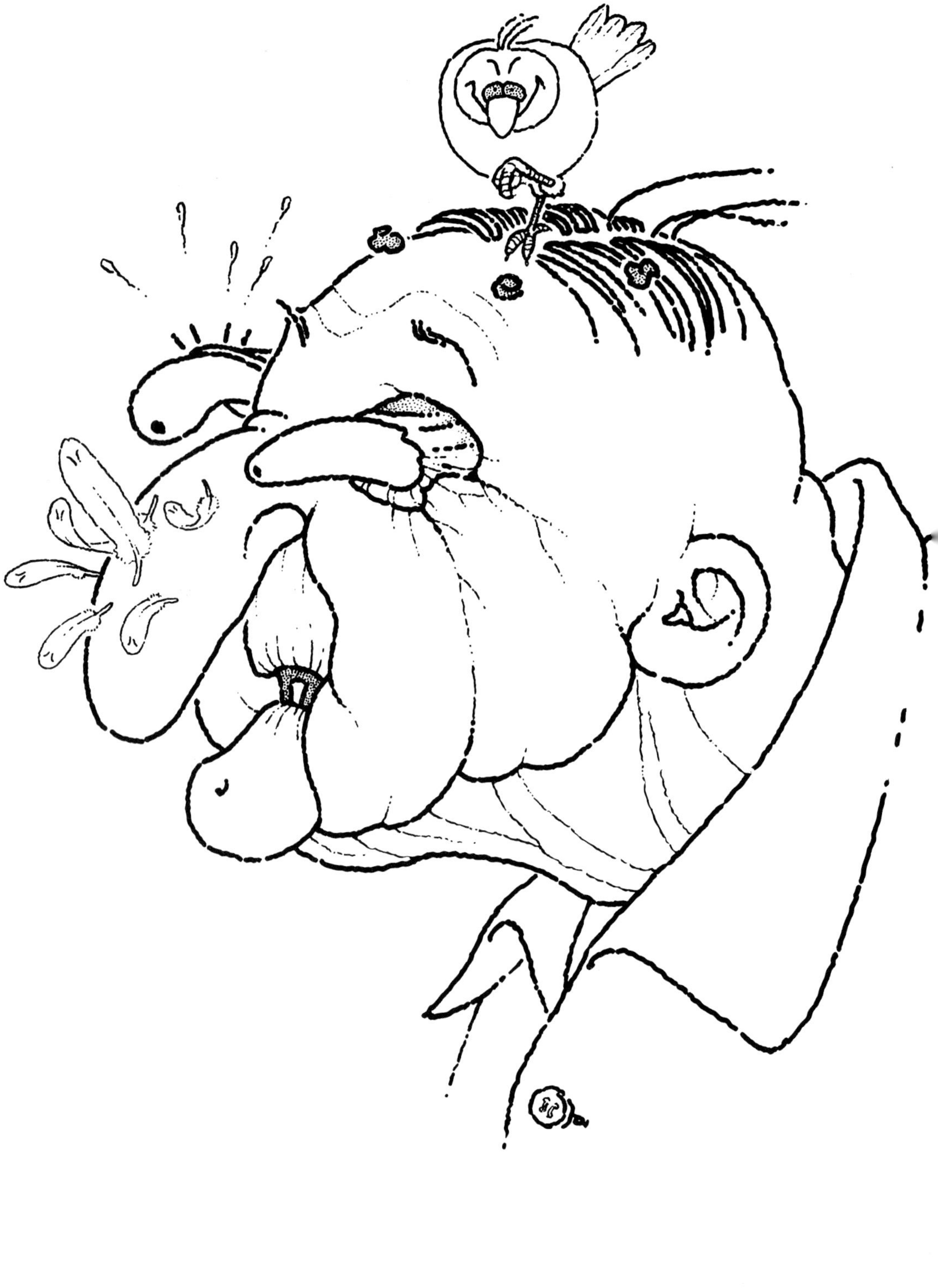

Ron Ellsworth was born and raised and received his art training in Los Angeles. He is otherwise normal. He grew up with his dog Tippy, also an Angelino. They were a boy and his dog for fifteen sweet and normal years. It wasn't until his college days away from L.A. that he drifted away from the norm and experimented with bugs. A cricket named Buster. He liked it. Then he tried a bird—a budgie named Bozo. He liked that too. And then he tried a cat named Sweetpea, and he liked that very much.

After receiving his M.A. in printmaking, Ron found his niche in illustration and has received many laurels. He married Suzanne, an Angelino, and tried a son, David, which he likes most of all. Today, Ron and his family have settled down to a normal life in Los Angeles with three abnormal cats. They hope some day to move from Los Angeles.